Advance Praise

This book is life-saving CPR training for nonprofits. An invaluable resource for the board or staff leader who takes their risk management responsibility seriously. The organization that takes advantage of Starr's extensive down-to-earth advice will prevent most "bad things" that could happen and will be ready to remedy the unpreventable crises.

—TIM WOLFRED, Senior Project Director, CompassPoint Nonprofit Services, author of *Managing Executive Transitions: a Guide for Nonprofits*

When Bad Thing Happen to Good Organizations *should have a prime place on every Executive Director's bookshelf! Starr Mayer offers straightforward, essential guidance to boards of nonprofits on how to avoid crises and how to deal effectively with crises that DO occur. ED's and Board members alike will sleep better at night because of this book.*

—BETH GREENLAND, Greenland & Associates, leadership coach and consultant to nonprofits

i

Passion, patience and perspective—the keys to any leader's credibility when facing a crisis. Starr Mayer's wise and thoughtful approach provides all three. With a contagious love of serving others, Starr lights the way through turmoil by keeping the organization's focus on its reason for being. Bad things do happen. Be prepared—read this book. When crisis hits, people will believe you when you say you know the way.

—Patrice Altenhofen, President,
Cascade Employers Association

Ms Mayer brings an enthusiasm of spirit to any task she undertakes and this book is no exception. A must read for any manager wanting to approach problem solving in a creative and productive way.

—Scot Dewhirst, Attorney at Law and Co-Director,
Center for Dispute Resolution, Capital University Law School

If your organization is experiencing a crisis, take heart. When Bad Thing Happen to Good Organizations *provides a comprehensive approach to get you through the short-term, and then shore up your organization for the future. For those who picked up this book as a proactive way to avoid catastrophe, you will find a rich set of resources for your board and staff-- through good times and bad. Starr Mayer has produced an important contribution to the literature on nonprofit management and governance.*

—Heather H. Iliff, Director, Consulting Group,
Maryland Nonprofits

Planning and preparation are extremely important for trying to prevent "bad things" from happening. And Ms Mayer is absolutely correct that effective conflict resolution skills are essential for the times when conflicts cannot be prevented. This book makes the case for prevention knowledge and resolution skills in practical ways.

—TERRY T. WHEELER, Attorney at Law, Past President, Association for Conflict Resolution

*After many years of serving on several nonprofit boards, I am happy to see that Ms Mayer has gathered important knowledge in this great book. Being a forensic accountant, I know for sure that bad things DO happen to good organizations. From my position as a board member, I urge you to read and absorb the information in the book; and **never, never** do nothing when you are faced with that bad thing.*

—K. D. BRICKER, CPA, DABFA, Senior Partner, Goodman and Company, LLP

If you have oversight of any size organization, you will find this a wonderful resource. Ms Mayer brings a long history of experience and wisdom to bear in this book. I appreciate the examples from a variety of settings. I will be using it in my ministry.

—REV. JAMES F. MAUNEY, Bishop, Virginia Synod of the ELCA

WHEN BAD THINGS HAPPEN TO GOOD ORGANIZATIONS

How Effective Managers Prepare for Crisis

STARR MAYER

MORGAN JAMES PUBLISHING • NEW YORK

WHEN BAD THINGS HAPPEN
TO GOOD ORGANIZATIONS

ISBN: 978-1-60037-861-4 (Paperback)
Library of Congress Control Number: 2010934839

Published by:
MORGAN JAMES PUBLISHING
1225 Franklin Ave Ste 32
Garden City, NY 11530-1693
Toll Free 800-485-4943
www.MorganJamesPublishing.com

Cover/Interior Design by:
Rachel Lopez
rachel@r2cdesign.com

Dedication

To the amazing women who offer a lifetime of professional and personal inspiration and support —my mother, Helen Wolle, and my sisters, Cherrie Brounstein, Pamela Pierce and Angela Wolle.

Contents

Acknowledgments

Working with nonprofit organizations is a privilege. Working with organizations in a time of crisis is a very special privilege. The stakes are high; skills are often at their best; trust is a necessity. I have spent my professional life working with universities, churches, and traditional nonprofit organizations as a consultant, a mediator, or a manager. I am appreciative of the insights of my colleagues and clients at each of my employment homes. I am particularly grateful for my time at Habitat for Humanity and my colleagues in the Risk Prevention and Response Unit. Amy Davies and Krista Padgett were trailblazers in this new unit and always had courage to spare. I also benefited from the various programs championed by the Virginia Synod of the Evangelical Lutheran Church of America. Participation in the programs they facilitated—like Healthy Congregations and BridgeBuilders—strengthened my understanding of organizations. Capital University's Center for Dispute Resolution, housed in the law school, was one of the first schools to create multiple mediation services for citizens. It has gone on to educate attorneys and lay professionals in mediation techniques not only in the United States but in many other countries. The core of who I became as a professional was forged at that school.

For this book I am particularly indebted to Janet V. Green, my colleague and friend and muse. Without her encouragement, the first word would not have been written. I appreciated the suggestions and support from Bob Yarbrough, a talented professional who was a keen reader and critic. My lifelong friend Karen Young inspired me with her day-to-day struggles as the president of a nonprofit board. Thanks to Beth Greenland and Cynthia Koch as well as to LaToya Parker and Katina Grays for improving the final product. There were numerous executive directors, board presidents, pastors, CEO's and CFO's who were generous with their time and their candor as they supplied fascinating examples of things gone wrong and things done right.

It was a gift to have Morgan James as the publisher and to have open access to David Hancock for instant answers and honest feedback.

My son Kevin Huffman works as executive vice president of a national nonprofit. He offered years of wisdom and humor as we discussed the world of nonprofits. My son Todd Huffman has coached and taught at private colleges, and I benefited from his observations about various managerial approaches. And I thank my patient husband who always believed in me and, more importantly, in us.

Introduction

In a time of crisis, no resource is so precious or so perishable as credibility.

—Karen Tumulty, *Washington Post*, June 6, 2010

All wise leaders of nonprofit organizations know they are just one crisis away from calamity. And in their heart of hearts, they know that averting a crisis is two parts luck for one part skill. When they ponder the unknowns, leaders wonder how they might cope with such a crisis. They know the fates of their organizations depend upon what happens after such an event, and they know it will be their responsibility to perform. Then the equation will rest more upon skill than luck.

This book is for wise leaders: those who want to sleep well at night and to face clients, donors, and volunteers with a clear vision. It is for those willing to take the identified steps to reduce the chances of a catastrophe and increase their competence and dexterity if a crisis comes.

The nonprofit institution, by definition and by description, has its own constraints and advantages. Although, technically, nonprofits include labor unions, charities, schools, churches, hospitals, foundations, and even art leagues, the reality is that charities, churches, and community groups function with structures and challenges similar to each other.

Many nonprofits have this in common:

- They operate on shoestring budgets.
- They are led by a board or council.
- They utilize volunteers in significant ways.
- They have relatively small staffs in proportion to the programs they operate.
- They have a mission.
- They depend upon public goodwill for their funding, their public relations, and their people.

Moreover, almost all nonprofits struggle with the same basic responsibilities:

- Fundraising
- Administering good programs
- Finding and retaining good people (staff, boards, members, volunteers, donors)
- Maintaining a positive public image

- Balancing the budget
- Maintaining a facility—whether owned or rented—so it is safe and functional

Without care and foresight, any of the constraints of trying to do too much with too few resources can result in both small problems and large, expensive crises. Reading the newspapers is a weekly reminder of nonprofits in trouble: misappropriated funds; sexual misconduct; internal but public board conflict; sequential staff turnovers; a death; a serious accident; a name that was trusted being tied to unsavory work.

This book is addressed to all leaders of churches and nonprofits: clergy, CEO's, board members, and executive directors. Together, board and staff must address the concerns raised in this book and ensure that the potential for crisis is at the forefront of the leadership agenda. Ultimately, though, it is the board or council that has the legal responsibility for the organization and is the employer of the paid staff. It is this collective group of leaders that must take the necessary steps to ensure the well being of the nonprofit, to protect its good name, and to guard its mission.

Peter Drucker, a voice of wisdom for the nonprofit world, acknowledged the lurking danger of crises in his book, *Managing the Nonprofit Organization: Principles and Practices*. Drucker describes leadership as a "Foul-Weather job":

Fortunately or unfortunately, the one predictable thing in any organization is the crisis. That always comes. That's when you DO depend on the leader.

The most important task of an organization's leader is to anticipate crisis. Perhaps not to avert it, but to anticipate it. To wait until the crisis hits is already abdication. One has to make the organization capable of anticipating the storm, weathering it, and in fact, being ahead of it ... You cannot prevent a major catastrophe, but you can build an organization that is battle-ready, that has high morale, and also has been through a crisis, knows how to behave, trusts itself and where people trust one another...

This book is for leaders who are ready to don the role of first responders—those who, when they put on the gear, understand the protocol which must be followed in the event of a disaster. There are many other books written by competent people to help nonprofits improve their capacity, develop their boards, increase their fundraising, and manage their staff more effectively. To the extent that this book touches on these topics, it is with the sole intent of preventing as many crises as possible and keeping those that happen from becoming life-threatening. If you are one of the three-parts lucky organizations who have never had a crisis—but you continue to work to address the key issues which might prevent crises—you can know you have built a stronger and healthier organization, one able to withstand any unforeseen events.

ABOUT CRISES

What actually constitutes a crisis? *For some it may be difficult to picture what events would necessitate thinking in crisis mode. Problem-solving is an ongoing duty for leaders, but once you have identified a crisis, a different level of action and planning must take place. Crises may be generated from outside the organization, such as by fire or flood or death; they may originate from within the organization with a financial crisis, embezzlement, or misconduct on the part of a leader. This chapter helps identify a true crisis and lays the groundwork for thinking about how to prevent, remedy, or repair the damage. The key is to focus on policies and on people.*

CHAPTER 1

Questions to Consider

s this a *crisis* or merely a problem to be addressed? Here are some defining questions to consider:

- Is this situation something the press might be interested in? If a story were published, would it be a threat to the organization?
- Does this situation involve
  - ✓ Money?
  - ✓ Sex?
  - ✓ Possible endangerment of a child or children?
- Does this situation represent a potential lawsuit, with the organization or its staff or board as plaintiffs or defendants?
- Does this situation threaten the organization's credibility?
- Does this situation threaten the organization's ability to exist?

Crises come in two forms: those that are external—usually acts of God or nature—and those that have an internal genesis. In either case, they must be addressed.

External Crises

All organizations are subject to the external crises that come with little or no warning and are not a result of negligence. While, in some cases, they can be anticipated and their damage somewhat mitigated (by insurance, safety measures, or training and policies), they are a risk. Fires, floods, and hurricanes fall into this category. Deaths caused by accident, suicide, or homicide fall into this category. A sudden illness—whether mental or physical—can be an externally caused crisis for an organization.

One nonprofit had a client who was murdered, and the death was linked to the organization in front page headlines, even though the assailant was unknown to anyone but the victim. Another organization had a volunteer who died from an aneurism while working at the program site. Hurricanes and floods have wiped out organizations' headquarters, the homes of their clients, the products of their volunteers' labors, and their vital records. For some organizations, such events delivered a fatal blow.

Internal Crises

This form of crisis cannot necessarily be anticipated but is created within the organization. The rule of thumb for identifying a terrible occurrence that can destroy an organization is this: It involves sex, money and/or harm to children. Worse, of course, is any combination of the three.

Any real *crime* connected to the nonprofit will cause unwanted attention and can create an immediate crisis.

What Makes a Crisis Life-Threatening

An organization's bread and butter is its reputation. This is especially true for nonprofits. A crisis at a for-profit organization has to be truly catastrophic for the world to take notice. Think of BP, Toyota, or AIG. But even a relatively small event in the life of a nonprofit can make the headlines and undermine public confidence. An embezzlement of as little as $500 has created a serious situation for small nonprofits. It is as true of organizations as it is of individuals: once a reputation is tainted and the public's faith is shaken, it is very difficult to rebuild trust. Carefully guarding that primary asset is the only responsible way to lead nonprofit organizations.

Anything that threatens the ability to continue functioning and meeting your mission is a crisis. If the organization has to lay off all staff; if there is no more money for program expenses; if donors determine the organization's cause to be suspect; if protests are set up and it is impossible to conduct business; if an unhappy board member, volunteer, or client decides to go to the media and give details of dishonesty or mistreatment of others—these are crises. As crises they must be addressed immediately by the full board of directors.

Prevention and Cure

Prevention is easier and cheaper than cure. So why doesn't every organization devote money, time, and personnel to preventing risk? Perhaps it's because the nonprofit world is full of optimists who think that, if the mission is laudable and leaders just do the best job possible, intentions will be rewarded and nothing bad will ever happen.

Organizations wish and hope that no bad things will occur. Then, when bad things do happen, they are sad and bewildered. How much better would it be if we could persuade people to provide for prevention?

The best way to prevent crises is to invest in:

POLICIES

PEOPLE

Almost every bad occurrence can be prevented, mitigated, or resolved with careful attention to having good *policies* and good *people*.

Often, conversations among those who care about nonprofit work center on which is more important—having good policies or finding the right leader. It is a chicken-or-egg question with no right answer. On the one hand, the first thing good leadership does is ensure there are solid organizational policies and systems. On the other hand, policies not only outlast the people in an organization— they create a climate that is attractive to the right people and which can help legitimately rid the organization of the wrong people.

Even with good people and good policies, crises may happen, and conflict will almost certainly occur. The key to healthy organizations is to have ways of dealing with crises and managing conflict, which can address or neutralize crises and turn potential risk into organizational benefit. Then policies and people become the cure.

The Keys to Crisis Management

- Understand what constitutes a crisis. (Chapter One)

- Mitigate the risk and impact of crises with policies and people. (Chapters Two and Three)

- Know when an incident or a culture is a precursor to a crisis. Knowing allows you to intervene proactively. Dealing with conflict well and early can turn a situation that might become a crisis into something positive. (Chapter Four)

- Handle an unexpected crisis in a timely and professional manner in order to minimize damage. (Chapter Five)

- Continue important repair work after the crisis. (Chapter Six)

- Plan for a crisis. Create a team to monitor and protect the agency in a continuous way and have a strategy to activate should a crisis appear. (Chapter Seven)

Many organizations have come through crises on the other side—some even stronger than before they went in—because they were honest in their assessment and intentional in their remedies.

PREVENTING CRISES WITH POLICIES

Most organizations have some policies.

Fewer organizations have a full manual of up-to-date policies with which everyone is familiar and which guide the work of the organization. Having such policies in place can prevent many of the missteps which could become crises. If a crisis occurs, policies let the public know that your management exercised foresight. Good policies can provide the sort of neutral programmatic guidance which is transparent, fair, and consistent. Policies create a more stable and pleasant work environment. While there may be magic in policies, there is no mystery in creating a solid base of important documents. All it takes is intentionality.

CHAPTER 2

What is a policy? Policies, procedures, guidelines, standards—all are board- or council-approved ways of operating that provide consistency to the way the nonprofit functions. Here is the fact: *Policies are your organization's friend.* They make organizational life easier. They allow the nonprofit to treat all situations and all persons the same—those they like and those they don't. An organization or its leaders can never be accused of playing favorites if the same documents are asked of all clients, the same policies are applied to all constituents, and the same rules govern all programs. All get the same treatment.

The Benefits of Policies

Policies are, of course, only as good as their application. Real policies don't just *allow* you to do the things mentioned above; they *require* you to do those things. Having policies that are ignored or applied inconsistently can have serious consequences.

11

In one example of policies ignored, a leader created a sense of disorder that was worse than not having policies in place. As the head of a nonprofit organization, he essentially wanted people to depend on him rather than on the structure of the organization. His door was always open. He made policy on the fly, and he also defied it. He was fond of what he called "one-offs"—which translated to his constantly making exceptions. Of course, this led to conflict and frustration on the part of those who saw themselves as not being favored. It also deprived the organization of the ability to set and follow precedents. Whether the one-offs were applied to individual staff or to branches of the organization, the unpredictability of the decisions made it hard for others to determine acceptable courses of action.

Policies must be enforced consistently, fairly, and transparently. When the culture of an organization is one of making decisions based on each individual situation, there will be generalized anxiety, paranoia, and accusations of bias. With good policies consistently applied, it is unlikely there will be validated claims of favor based upon age, gender, race, language, or favoritism. There will also be a culture of predictability and focus, because people aren't uncertain about what is expected of them or what they can expect from their organization.

Policies rise above personalities and focus on the organization. Talking about policies and referencing them frequently allows all of those connected with the nonprofit to likewise focus on the organization and not on the individuals who make up the organization *at this particular time*. Policies, while they can and should be updated, are timeless. They are not developed for those who are currently board members, volunteers, staff members, clients, or members. Rather, they are based upon organizational health and apply to all of those who may be in those positions in the future.

Policies can, interestingly, prevent many interpersonal conflicts, because they depersonalize much of the decision making. Those who want special treatment will find there is a standard answer to be found in the policies. Without that standard, the grapevine operates quickly to allow constituents to know when exceptions have been made so that they feel entitled to similar treatment.

The board will not be inclined to waive their policy regarding conflict of interest because their new board chair is a member of the state legislature and will be able to make things happen that will help the organization. The policy requiring a criminal background check before working with children won't be waived because "we've known his family for generations."

Determining Which Policies Are Needed

Most organizations—especially those that are young or small or both—don't think about policies until they need one. That's okay. Figuring out a policy after a crisis or question will still be useful the next time. And there will be a next time. Every time a difficult decision is made, it is useful to think about what has been learned and, if appropriate, to draft a policy for the board to approve and apply when similar questions arise.

There is no reason to labor over creating policy on your own, when there are numerous samples of every imaginable policy available online. Some samples are available at the website linked to this book. The very best sources, however, are a nonprofit's parent organization and/or a sister organization which is similar in size and purpose.

Established foundations sometimes have model documents which they make available. Some collective organizations, such as the Maryland Association of Nonprofit Organizations, have standards, policies, and trainings. These can be adapted to each group or church with minimum effort. It is important to view them with a critical eye and make sure they meet the particular needs of a specific organization and its mission and programs.

The Essential Documents for a Policy Manual

By-Laws

Included in by-laws are such important details as information about board meetings and officers, minimal job descriptions, nomination processes for board members, term limits, the reporting relationship of the paid staff, etc.

Personnel Manual

If you have more than one employee, this is important. A personnel policy covers hiring, firing, dress, hours, payment logistics, disciplinary actions, appeals, etc.

Fiscal Management

How money is handled is vitally important to an organization's integrity. Nonprofits must have a system of checks and balances—and segregation of duties—built into policy. If the organization is over a certain size, or receives money from organizations such as

United Way or requires this in by-laws, it will be necessary to have an outside audit or a financial review annually. How does the paid staff who handles money relate to the board or council treasurer? If there is a bookkeeping person or firm, how do they fit with staff and board responsibilities? These are questions that need to be answered.

Communication Policy

At any given time, only one person should speak on behalf of the organization. This should be a key component of a communication policy, which describes the role of board and staff when communicating outside the organization. This is a vital document to have in place during a crisis.

Conflict of Interest Policy

This policy ensures that the board and staff will put the interests of the nonprofit first and will not profit from their connection with the organization. Most policies specify that anyone paid by the organization cannot be on the board. A key component is full disclosure of the outside interests of board members and staff.

Safety

Safety policies focus on the facility, personnel, and program sites. Therefore, if the church operates a day care center, safety policies will address criminal background checks for staff, safety of play equipment, etc. Policy will also include procedures for what to do in case of an emergency.

Information Technology Protection

Determine in detail who has access to what information, what back-ups will be mandatory, how often passwords will be changed, what web browsing is permissible, and what oversight can be expected.

Succession Plan

While it is often said that no one is irreplaceable, that is not always true. It is surely not true if there is no plan for an individual's unexpected departure. Before determining how to substitute for an individual's work, it is necessary to know what their responsibilities actually are. Whether board or staff, every person must have an understudy.

Once, when giving a workshop about succession planning, I asked what the attendees' organizations would do if their executive director were hit by a bus. A hand in the front row went up, and the woman said she was that very person.

She had left her office for a cup of coffee mid-morning and was hit by a bus. And, no, they didn't have a plan in place.

It is important to be able to function in the face of unknowns like long-term illness, precipitous resignations, and even deaths. There are many sample succession plans available which can be adapted to different organizations.

Emergency Contingency Plan

In the appendix, there is a six-month plan to guide a board through the process of gathering information and turning it into the intelligence necessary to confront a crisis. It is a relatively painless process which will create compounded peace of mind for the leadership of the organization.

Depending upon the work done by the nonprofit, there may be other vital policies. An organization with a large endowment may want an investment policy. A group with a high value name may need a policy to define when they will allow their name to be attached to other products or groups.

Policies complement the legal requirements which every nonprofit must meet, including those specific to the program areas. For example, all Habitat houses must be built to local code and then inspected; and day care centers must be licensed.

What is a policy? Policies, procedures, guidelines, standards—all are board- or council-approved ways of operating that provide consistency to the way the nonprofit functions. The above list of policy manual essentials is just a beginning. Best practices might include a manual for office procedure and up-to-date job descriptions. Good policy-makers ask themselves, *If the office manager were taken ill, would we know what to do, where things are, what insurance is in place, or how to open files?*

Policies Are Often Overlooked

It's difficult to understand why every nonprofit doesn't have and adhere to policies. It seems that, for many people, they are too busy managing the day-to-day business to take time out to think about policies. If policies aren't already in place, it feels overwhelming to create them; if they do exist, reviewing them feels confounding. Also, for some people in the nonprofit world, having policies makes things seem impersonal and cold. They think of themselves as being more nimble and people-friendly if they don't have all of those "rules." Unfortunately, the rules have come to be seen as something entirely divorced from the organization's commitment to mission. Policy must be part of our compassionate attention to the work we do. It does not have to be inflexible. It is far easier, however, to make an exception to a policy for a well-defined reason, than to make a hundred individual decisions based upon different stories, rationales, and points of reference.

Here's a classic tale of how things snowball and how a policy—in the best sense of being impersonal—could have saved everyone serious organizational conflict. A gentleman who had been on a council for a long time asked to use the credit card to purchase some items for the next congregational event. When the event had concluded, questions were raised about the amount spent, but few details were offered. Later, when conflicts began to erupt in the council and factions appeared, money became the focus. Old receipts were collected, and on a Wal-Mart bill was an item for "pleated pants," which the council member had charged on the church credit card. When discussed later, it was acknowledged that there were no guidelines established for reimbursement, no policies regarding use of the credit card, what items could be purchased, or proof of purchase. Further, at the time, no one wanted to ask the gentleman for his receipt, because it seemed to suggest distrust. Policies could have prevented the incident, as well as the furor and frustration that came afterwards. This one incident caused a complete realignment of the board. People left; those who remained were full of misgivings; and new people were difficult to recruit.1

Part of the policy dilemma is that organizations are constantly in motion. Making adjustments to them is like changing a tire on a moving vehicle. Creating a solid body of policies requires intentionality. This book is a plea for that commitment. It provides a road map to guide groups to safety.

It would be naïve to believe that having the right policies solves each and every problem, but policies speak to the professionalism of even small organizations. Policies create boundaries. Most organizations and individuals benefit from clear boundaries. Other times, those guidelines help resolve contentious issues. Not wanting to hurt someone's feelings is exactly why having policies works. Everyone is expected to present receipts for purchases in order to receive a reimbursement. It doesn't matter how long someone has been a volunteer or whether everyone trusts him or no one trusts him. A receipt is expected and required. End of story. In the case of the church mentioned above, fifteen minutes of board conversation and a written policy would have saved the group from months of haggling and bad feelings.

Thinking of the definitions of crises, it is clear that many problems could be prevented or mitigated by good board-approved policies which are routinely applied.

Examples of Preventing Crises with Policies

A community hospital decided to hire a new group of anesthesiologists. They needed to do this before the contract with the current group of professionals expired, so they hurriedly contracted with a group in another state without appropriate vetting. The newspapers heard complaints from the ousted group and did their own investigation. They found that the new group of health practitioners had only been in business for a few months and had falsified their history. Furthermore, their information regarding their address and contacts was false. The hospital was not only forced to answer public questions about their policies and procedures, but they had to cancel surgeries over a several-month period as they scrambled to find a new group of doctors and nurses. Their lack of protocol regarding contracts, hiring, firing, and standards for personnel was more damaging than being unable to perform their work. Policies would have prevented this crisis from happening.

A university had a sudden financial crisis stemming from the banking and economic crisis afflicting the whole country. The school's communication policy mandated clear and open communication between the president and everyone in the school's extended family. The messages sent by mail and e-mail, and those delivered in meetings, were consistent: Here are the things we are doing to address this crisis; we will continue to inform you of our situation and our responses; there is no danger of redundancies at this time; we see a recovery within the next six months. Their policy allowed them not only to avert a crisis but to build a community of committed students, donors, faculty, and townspeople who felt triumphant when the situation turned around.

A very small nonprofit, which devoted itself to helping cancer patients, demonstrated an amazing level of sophistication regarding policies. Although their office staff consisted of only three workers, and their board numbered fifteen, they nevertheless enacted a full component of appropriate policies. One of those was ultimately significant for them. It was, they said, their new auditor who insisted on looking over their investment policies. In spite of their small size, the organization was funded by a sizeable endowment. Knowing how important their investment portfolio was to them, the board had passed policies that derivatives would be disallowed and that they would never hold investments in companies such as tobacco companies, which might undermine their mission. The new auditor read every mutual fund description and found a fund which violated that policy. Many for-profit and nonprofit companies must wish they had been so wise as to avoid derivatives. But this group was also sensitive to how the public might have reacted if they had discovered investments in products causing cancer.

An executive director noted, not uncharacteristically, "I don't like management letters," referring to the memos from audit firms to boards of directors. But she took note when her board received word that there were three areas of material deficiency; they vowed to address every weakness. That action allowed them to weather the unforeseen death of their bookkeeper and to receive a clean bill of health when the next audit came around. Their policies were developed to ensure healthy financial accounting. This board has become converts to the value of good policies.

Many nonprofit organizations have decided to hitch their wagons to a for-profit "star" by doing "cause-related marketing." Businesses are eager to piggy back on the credibility of nonprofit causes. Nonprofits, always needing financial security, have sometimes been tempted to form partnerships without checking the products they appear to be endorsing. Straight from old news reports comes this cautionary tale: "On July 31, 1988, the American Medical Association announced it would pay $9.9 million to the Sunbeam Corporation to settle a breach of contract suit … The suit was filed in September, 1978, after the AMA announced it would not honor an exclusive five-year royalty agreement under which the AMA logo would have been placed on Sunbeam's 'Health at Home' products, which included heating pads and humidifiers. The endorsement plan, which had no requirement that the AMA test the products, was widely criticized by ethicists, physicians, and newspaper editorialists who accused the AMA of compromising its credibility ... An investigative report on the management decisions leading to the contract led the AMA's chief executive officer and two other top AMA executives to resign. The trustees also appointed a task force to develop standards for future business arrangements."2

After severe flooding in many parts of the country, several nonprofits found that having their important documents—whether related to the organization, their facility, or their clients—stored in fire and water-proof locations saved their organizational lives. Other nonprofits lost every important document in flooding and spent countless days and dollars recreating things. Some never recovered from the disaster. For those organizations that survived, protecting documents became mandated policy.

Thinking of policies as an integral part of the fabric of the organization can be the impetus for creating a good policy manual. Policies may sound like words on paper or like an exercise to complete and file and forget. In fact, policies become like a mediator or judge; they become the objective, neutral "other" in the life of the organization. Having good policies frees the people of the organization to do the work they have chosen to do and to do it more confidently and competently.

PREVENTING CRISES WITH PEOPLE

Nonprofits have two groups of people—
a board of directors or church council and a staff—who provide leadership to the organization. They also represent their organizations to the public in essential ways. It is imperative that these people be carefully selected, managed in ways that bring out their best qualities, and moved out of the organization when their time of productive service is complete. Good people with good judgment, strong values, and the right skills protect the organization over and over again from harm. Having an effective board and staff who work well together comes only from constantly surveying the roles, tasks, and competence of the organization's people.

CHAPTER 3

Given the importance most professionals place upon people (often picturing a single charismatic leader, and usually thinking of them as far more important than policies), it is hard to understand why so many nonprofits treat the care and feeding of their people in such a casual manner. They hope the right people will arrive, fully trained and focused, at the right time. They hope the right people will stay and the wrong people will decide on their own to leave. They hope people will do their work well and represent the organization admirably. For many organizations it is difficult to take any time out to allow for careful planning for the effective use of people, just as it is difficult to create a policy framework. When an organization is under pressure, there is no time to effect change. "No time" is the constant mantra heard within most nonprofits. But as a friend always says, "If you don't have time to do it right, when will you have time to do it over?" Crises sap energy and time. So it is incumbent upon us to give careful thought to people, and do the foundational work for change now.

The key to having good people is intentionality—a variation of what is required to have solid policies. It requires a framework for thinking about the people who represent your organization to the public. If it's about finding only *perfect* people for board, staff, or volunteer positions, there will be no pool to choose from. If it's about finding *great* people for every single spot, everyone will be competing for those same people. As Donald Rumsfeld said, "You go to war with the army you have; not the army you might want or wish to have." In order for people to be a bulwark against crises, organizations must pick the best people, using the best processes. They must manage those people in the most effective way. And they must get rid of those who aren't working well. That's true for every position in the organization. Great people are assets; good people are sometimes assets; the wrong people are liabilities.

The People Who Make Up the Board of Directors

Many people who work with nonprofits feel that boards are a perplexing element inherited from the for-profit world. Now, of course, they are an accepted part of nonprofits, and it is too late to think about whether they really fit. But it is not too late to think about how they must add value to the organizations they serve. Consider the facts about board members:

- They volunteer their time. As with other volunteers, they serve at their own pleasure. If their board membership ceases to meet their individual needs they can simply resign or stop functioning effectively.

- They have other responsibilities. Most board members are chosen for their professional skills and their roles as community leaders. Their time is limited. If they are able to prepare for a board meeting by thinking about the issues ahead of time and, if they can focus during the meeting and bring those professional and leadership skills to the table, then they have been well chosen.

- They meet only once a month. Sometimes they meet less than that. Sometimes members miss a meeting. Checking into the important workings of an organization on such an irregular basis makes thoughtful and informed decision-making difficult.

- They are often uneducated about the mission and the day-to-day functioning of the organization, even though they have been tasked with planning, budgeting, and providing oversight.

- They are reliant on the paid staff to guide them by highlighting areas of concern; and, yet, collectively, they are the bosses, the managers of the chief executive.

- They often have not served on nonprofit boards before and are uncertain of their role. Even if they have been on other boards, the maturity of the organization determines whether a board is considered a working board or a governing board. Expectations for board members are very different depending on the group, and those expectations are not necessarily made clear.

• They work with a changing roster of members. Hopefully, the changes are somewhat predictable, but the group itself is not a static part of the organization.

The Role of the Board

Having a highly functioning board of bright and committed individuals is, sadly, the exception rather than the norm. And yet a good board that understands its role, is connected to the community, and believes in the mission of the organization can make all the difference in the health of that organization.

Too often board members are haphazardly chosen in a process that has not been spelled out. Their jobs are not defined. Their roles, vis-a-vis the staff, are blurred. The staff vacillates between asking too much of board members and asking too little. There is little to no training for board members. Even if, serendipitously, good people are brought onto a board, there may have been little thought for how that board comes together as a unit. The fact that these boards and councils function at all is a miracle. What is sobering is looking at what is *legally* expected of a board for a nonprofit. Boards are fiscally and legally responsible for the organization. Their allegiance is to the overall church or organization. Their loyalty should not be to any individual, be it pastor, priest, rabbi, or CEO. And they must understand and protect the organization fiscally. This means that not only the treasurer must understand the money that comes in and goes out. The board as a whole must be knowledgeable. It is clearly too large a responsibility for random selections of random people made in order to fulfill some magic number of ideal membership. The relevance to the prevention of crises is obvious. A strong board is a bulwark against problems; a weak board may become its own liability. It is also true that, because of the changing nature of board memberships, strong boards tend to breed strong boards, and weak boards can breed generations of weak boards.

What can nonprofits do to cultivate and protect the important asset of a strong board and thus prevent or mitigate some crises?

Keys to Creating a Highly Functioning Board

- Be clear about the role of the board and the roles of individual board members. The board as a unit is responsible for the defined tasks; the board as a whole manages the executive. Individual board members function effectively as part of the whole and in their defined roles as committee chairs or members.

- Be clear about the role of board committees. Committees can veer off course and create unintended liability for the board and the organization. This problem can be minimized by defining links of communication and delineating authority.

- Identify professional expertise that is important to the organization. Most nonprofits want someone with legal knowledge and financial expertise. Diversity almost always strengthens a group's decision-making ability by putting different approaches to problems on the table. Many organizations bring individuals onto a board in an ad hoc way—either to replace someone who has left or because it is that time of year. Mature organizations know what they need in this important group of leaders, and they spend months developing a plan for the board, as well as months cultivating potential board members.

- Even the best individuals need to understand what is expected of them. Before inviting someone to join the board or council, a clear job description should be shared. This would spell out any commitments— in terms of time and money—in a way that neither underplays nor exaggerates the expectations. Good people respond well to this. If this process of selection is handled lazily, it will produce lazy board members.

- Even the best individuals need a good orientation to the organization they are joining in order to competently fulfill their job as board member. This orientation will cover the national/international organization, the work which the local nonprofit undertakes, the financial picture, clients, committee structure, and any challenges which lie ahead. A good board orientation will show working documents which previous boards or councils have developed, like strategic plans, budgets, and policies.

- Even the best individuals can wander off course if there isn't strong leadership in the form of a president or chair. Good board/council leadership is even-handed. A leader controls the agenda but not the outcome. Good leaders encourage debate and discussion but discourage arguments or dissent that can become conflict. If conflict does arise, a good leader acknowledges the tension, identifies the components, and lays out a path to resolution.

- A good board is clear about their roles as board members, as compared to the roles of staff. They understand the role of the executive director or pastor, and they know that they are not individual bosses, but a collective manager. Clarifying distinctions between board and staff must be an on-going process.

Areas of Board Vulnerability

Where do boards go wrong? How can they morph from being a force for good to causing a crisis or being idle bystanders ignoring danger signs as the organization veers off course? Most by-laws or board job descriptions identify ways to avoid the worst of the problems. Here are the rules that help support the right people on your board of directors or church council.

Term limits

Term limits are usually defined in the by-laws and frame the term of a board member's service. Usually, terms are two or three years. Term limits specify whether a board member can serve more than one term and, if so, what limits the length of time a board member can serve. As a rule, this concept often draws resistance from board and staff alike. Here are some of the most frequently mentioned concerns:

- An organization might lose its best people.
- It is difficult to recruit new people.
- It is especially difficult to recruit new people with specific skills such as attorneys or accountants.
- The board may already have achieved a sort of balance or chemistry that is productive and might be upset by change.
- Institutional memory resides in board members who have served over a longer period of time.

These are legitimate concerns. There are also important rebuttals born out of painful experience:

- Generally, good people are not lost in this process of term limits or retained when it is ignored. Good people who are also highly committed to the organization will find other ways to make their contribution. Too often, lazy or indifferent folks overstay their welcome when term limits are not enforced.

- Good professionals can recommend other good professionals, often from the same firm. Sometimes a junior partner in a law firm or accounting practice has a bit more time and more energy to devote to the organization's work.

- Sometimes groups that get used to working together become *too* comfortable. This can be a liability. They don't challenge each other. Sometimes a small group of people takes over a board or council and this small group of people directs every decision. Sometimes groups become exclusive rather than inclusive, even when they don't intend to, and they begin to look the same in terms of age, gender, race, religion, or politics.

- The very act of searching for new potential board members changes the way an organization functions. If they are in recruitment mode year round, the organization will see volunteers and community leaders in a different way. Furthermore, as they are telling others the story of their nonprofit, they may recruit persons who may not be interested in immediate board membership, but may think about it later or recommend the organization to others.

- Institutional memory is important. So is a fresh approach. Board turnover ensures a balance of those who remember what was tried in the recent past and those who come at things with a blank slate and new ideas.

Aside from the good that comes from adding new people to the mix, there is the reality that people get tired. Rarely do people feel comfortable saying they have lost enthusiasm. And tired people do not make good decisions. Having term limits is an effective way to allow people to leave an organization while they feel good about the work they did. A sharp, fresh board with a professional approach to their important tasks is a guard against crises.

Nepotism

Never retain two people related by blood or marriage on the board or staff at the same time. There are arguments against this rule:

- People are always certain they can handle the inherent tensions or conflicts that may arise.

- Organizations sometimes build in firewalls—when staff or board members are related—to ensure there is not a direct reporting relationship.

- People who are committed to the organization devote a great deal of time to it, so they want to be able to share that commitment time with family.

The reality is that having two people related to each other as part of the same nonprofit leadership (board and/or staff) unbalances things in a way that is difficult to identify and more difficult to remedy. When considering the board as a fortress against crises, consider these factors:

- Even if the two family members think they can manage their work and their relationship, conflicts or crises which are part of nonprofit life will strain it. Even if the two people in question can conduct themselves professionally, others may not perceive them as being independent of each other and may perceive them as a voting block.

- Firewalls may work technically, but the perception may be that people are aligned or, at the least, are discussing things with each other.

- Relationships change. A divorce or rift in a relationship cannot help but impact others who are part of the same team.

- Being heavily invested in a church or other nonprofit organization only intensifies the opportunities for tensions and conflicts. The picture most people have of sharing the same passionate focus is rarely the way things play out. Whether the two people who are related agree or disagree, the chemistry of the organization is changed.

It is a rare organization that can absorb two people who are related. Small nonprofits and churches are especially vulnerable to being toppled by this undistributed weight. It is much better to avoid the situation altogether by having a policy which is enforced.

Conflicts of Interest

Adopt a strong conflict of interest policy, discuss it frequently, and adhere to it religiously. Board members want to help. They are willing to volunteer their services or try to get their friends, family, and professional colleagues involved with the organization. Sometimes that enthusiasm leads to decisions that may provide financial benefit to those same people. The question for the board is whether it occurs at the expense of the organization. Having a conflict of interest policy creates a good floor for everyone to stand upon. A good policy will offer a process for determining if, in fact, a conflict of interest exists, how members must remove themselves from decision-making, and how to address violations.

Almost every board-related crisis could have been avoided by attending to the recruitment, training, and management of good board members. Nonprofits should pay particular attention to those policies that apply to boards given their pivotal role.

Examples of Preventing Crises through Board Excellence

A nonprofit had been functioning with the same basic board of directors for many years. In theory, they complied with their by-laws as it related to term limits. In practice, they rotated familiar people on and off the board, often substituting husbands and wives, in order to maintain the same leadership group. They functioned like a social club. When the executive director, who had been uncomfortable with this practice but had not objected, left, the new executive director called attention to the risk this created for the organization. This initiated a revolving door of staff leadership and culminated in a crisis caused by the board's distraction and its inattention to programmatic flaws. A legal case ensued because of the programmatic crisis. Still, the board continued to point fingers at staff until they lost so many people that programming ceased.

A nonprofit organization had an executive director whose mother was the board president. The board had considered this situation and made arrangements for someone else on the board, not the mother, to be the liaison and manager of the executive director. A staff issue came up, and the members of staff were not able to resolve it directly with the executive director. Eventually, the staff went, en masse, to the local newspaper. While, in theory, they might have been able to utilize their board intermediary, they lacked confidence that the board would be able to listen to their complaints about their executive director with an open mind. This became a front page story which made the organization vulnerable in other areas of business.

A church found out it was facing a financial shortfall. The pastor offered to loan the congregation his salary in order to be helpful. This created an awkward situation in which the council then owed money to the person they, in effect, supervised. When his performance began to decline, the council felt they could not require accountability. When the circumstances came to light, a crisis of confidence—both internal and external—ensued.

A committee of the board came upon information about property which could be purchased at what they felt was a bargain price. They met and determined to sign a contract to purchase the piece of land. When the board met, they were not only concerned with the high sales price; they clearly stated that there was no money in the budget and that purchase of the land did not fit into the strategic plan which the board had approved. When an attorney looked at the by-laws, she determined no board committee was authorized to purchase land. This led to serious rifts, since members of the committee felt their personal integrity had been compromised when they had to renege on agreements with people in the community. The board of directors felt the committee had jeopardized the organization with a decision the board saw as inappropriate and irresponsible.

One executive said, "The nominating committee is the most important part of the organization. Why don't all boards realize this? They are what bring the diversity and talent to the leadership."

Staff of Nonprofit Organizations

The CEO or executive director of a nonprofit is selected by the board of directors. Hiring and managing the chief of the nonprofit is arguably the most important job the board of directors undertakes. The CEO or executive director hires and manages the program staff for the organization. The staff manages the day-to-day operations of nonprofits, while the board sets the priorities, develops and oversees the budget, and performs long-term planning. Board members, director, and staff must work collaboratively.

Consider what we know about those who staff nonprofits:

- They are likely paid less than their counterparts at for-profit companies.
- They are probably part of a small staff or may even be the only paid staff.
- They wear many hats, whether fundraising, program-directing, or public relations.
- They work with volunteers.
- They operate with small budgets.
- Their office space is probably less than ideal.
- They have contact with the public.
- What they do influences how the community perceives the organization and whether or not they contribute to the organization.
- They work with boards.

Guidelines for Creating a Strong Staff

What can organizations do to ensure that their staff is an asset and not a liability? What can be done to retain staff who are able to prevent or mitigate crises?

Hire well. Take the time to know what is needed in a position, to advertise broadly, to interview well, and to do appropriate background and reference checks. There are many great resources for this process, in the form of both written materials and professional consultants. When a vacancy is created or a position developed, some organizations panic. A vacancy, however, is an opportunity to rethink. It is a time to evaluate whether, in Jim Collins' *Good to Great* vernacular, you have the right people sitting on the seats of the bus. Perhaps this is an opportunity to reduce your personnel. Perhaps this is a time to increase the numbers. It is definitely a time to re-evaluate.

Take time to do an organizational assessment. Some boards are in a hurry to find someone—especially if they are looking for a leader, such as an executive director or clergy. They may be nervous about who will do the work while the position is vacant, and they are often concerned that they themselves will have to manage tasks for which they are unprepared. They skip the process of self-assessment that would help them determine the organization's current and future needs, which could produce a job description that would meet those needs.

Open the search. Some organizations are concerned about being stuck with someone who isn't a fit. So they look for people who are known quantities— board members, those already on staff, or people in the community. In this state of mind, they are only looking at people who are currently available and whose work they generally know (but often in a limited way). Some worry about the public knowing about their vacancy. Others are concerned that too many people will apply and the process will overwhelm them. These are understandable concerns, but manageable challenges, and worth the effort it takes to address them.

Carefully consider "inside" candidates. Sometimes there is an inside candidate whom the organization knows and feels could move easily into the newly created position. Having that person apply and compete with others who are interested and capable can only be a positive experience for the organization and the candidate. Often, search committees are surprised by the high caliber of other applicants. If an inside candidate does not go through this process, they may lose credibility in the eyes of their current peers, just as they gain respect if they run the obstacle course that other nominees are asked to complete. It is also true that the search process—the interviews and the conversations with references—almost always gives new perspectives to the board and its search committee.

Have a process which is fair and transparent for all. Have a plan and a script for your process, from the point of advertising through the negotiation with the final candidate. Not having a plan can sow dissent in the organization for years to come, not to mention leading to the wrong decision.

Contact all references. Do background checks with an understanding of what is and is not acceptable to the organization, what is and is not important. Call the final candidates' references and ask good questions that are important to your organization. Pay attention to what is revealed. Sometimes people get sloppy at the end of the search. They are tired. They are eager to have the solution in their grasp. Sometimes their hearts are set on a candidate, and they really don't want to hear any negative information others might offer. Try to stay focused up until the end. Agree at the beginning of the process that it would be better to start over than to pick the wrong person.

Address any past organizational problems. Do this before bringing in someone new. Sometimes these problems were the reason the last person left; sometimes there are more recent problems which have cropped up during a vacancy. Asking a new person to enter an organization and immediately resolve problems is unrealistic and creates unnecessary burdens for everyone.

Be clear. Communicate to the new hire what is expected, the reporting channels, and the desired methods of sharing information.

Executive Transition Management

The process known as Executive Transition Management is a system to assist organizations when they move from one leader to another or when they hire their first full time executive. It provides a guide to a thoughtful search process which begins with an organizational assessment.

A good tool in the midst of a CEO vacancy is to appoint an intentional interim. Many church denominations have a cadre of people whose sole function is to serve in that capacity for congregations that are between pastors. Some organizations also supply interim executives to nonprofits. Having an interim who is decidedly not interested in the permanent position frees the board or council from the day-to-day responsibilities, while maintaining organizational stability during the search. There are several resources mentioned at the end of this book. As with the search for new board members, so a lazy search for the top leader will result in a lazy leader who leads in a lazy fashion. This is important whether the position being filled was held by a strong leader or a weak leader.

ETM is essential when an organization's founder is being replaced. Many articles have been written about Founder Syndrome and the peculiar difficulties created for board and staff when the founder of a nonprofit or church leaves. This situation suggests multiple tasks which often seem counter-intuitive or conflicting, such as honoring the past while making efforts to secure an independent path to the organization's future. The elements of ETM can guide an organization through this thicket of challenges.

Guidelines for Effective Management of Staff

Evaluate regularly—formally and informally. Do performance evaluations in a way that has already been explained at hiring and is clear, fair, and consistent from year to year and employee to employee. Begin with a ninety-day evaluation after hiring, and establish the practice of candid conversations between the chief executive/pastor and the board or council liaisons. Vow to address issues early and often, without allowing ill feelings to grow.

Manage people in a way that prevents small errors in judgment from becoming big mistakes. At the first sign that things are not going as well as expected, face the issues. Do not hope that hints will be received or problems ignored will go away. During conversation, state what is wanted along with what is not wanted. Be very specific and descriptive. Articulate concerns. Set a time to talk again and see if things have improved. When experience shows performances of staff have improved, it will be because of hard work on the part of both parties and frequent, candid conversations.

Write it down. If, as a manager, you are concerned about something, make and file notes about what has happened, what was discussed, what the response was, and what follow-up is expected. If the problem never arises again, great!

Fire sooner rather than later. Once relationships sour or work performance declines, situations rarely get better on their own. No one ever says, "I wish I'd waited longer to fire Mary/Joe." Having an unhappy, disruptive, or incompetent employee in the workforce—especially in a nonprofit workplace where every job is important—is toxic. If that person is the leader of the workforce, close attention is vital. Ignoring the work or attitude of a poor employee sends a bad message to other employees. They may think no one is paying attention or that the behavior is acceptable. Either unintended message may court conflict and possible crisis.

Have a good personnel policy. Be certain your employees are clear about its contents. This is a safeguard for all. Follow every step of your policy if someone is to be hired or fired. Sometimes an employee may have a particular skill or may be unusually talented, but he or she is also a source of staff conflict. In interviews, managers may talk about the dilemma of deciding when the negatives outweigh the positives. Is it possible that the loss of a particular talent or level of productivity might be outweighed by the improved performance of a team of people?

Keep good people happy. Turnover is costly in many ways. A vacancy at the top is a potential crisis. Often, so much attention is paid to the hiring phase or to addressing problems, that a board or organization overlooks the importance of keeping good people happily employed. Pay attention and make sure the executive—and others— know this is a priority.

While nonprofits have financial constraints, there are many perks which can be offered to executives as incentives or simply as singular expressions of appreciation. Many a contract for a desired leader has died because of what was perceived as a miserly or mean-spirited approach to benefits. Likewise, when working with an executive whom the organization wants to keep, be generous in the ways it is possible to be generous, i.e., vacation time, flexible hours, sabbaticals, and professional development.

When organizations get off track with their staffs and create issues which become organizational crises, it is because they sometimes get caught up in the day-to-day chaos that is part of the nonprofit world. They don't create opportunities to evaluate their plans, their people, the tasks they do, and the culture they have developed. There are hundreds of books written about people management. Human resources is an area of professional expertise. We include this section about staff in this book about crises, because hiring the wrong person can make an organization vulnerable. Not managing issues as they arise creates a breeding ground for conflict. Failure to fire people, when appropriate, can lead to crises.

Examples of Preventing Crises through Staff Excellence

A nonprofit was describing the time when a staff member—who had been in the office since the organization began—left suddenly with a major illness. The organization was clearly thrown into disarray. They did not want to have a long period of uncertainty with tasks left undone, so they quickly grabbed someone at the suggestion of a board member. Unfortunately, it was only a matter of weeks before they realized this was not the right match of person to job. Fortunately, they did not compound their error. They dismissed the person; and now, years later, they are pleased to retain their second choice. They understand clearly that they were fortunate to have bounced back from their selection of the wrong person. They learned a lesson, which they applied to the second, successful search and to subsequent job openings.

Another nonprofit was confused that, although their programs were doing everything intended and public image was high, staff morale was lower than it had ever been. Assuming there was something strategic that needed to change, the organization hired consultants to interview staff, hoping to create a realignment which would fix this low-grade infection evidenced by employees. What they learned was that one person who supervised others consistently undermined the work, the job satisfaction, and the productivity of those who reported to him. It was a simple matter to recommend firing that person. Once he had been removed, other evidence of his mismanagement became apparent. Morale returned to normal, and the decision to let him go was validated.

An organization advertised for their CEO and found out that a board member and a current staff person had applied, along with a large contingent of others. In the absence of a leader, the organization was overstretched. Rather than follow a protocol for selection, the board set up interviews at the mercy of board members' schedules. Consequently, not every person on the search committee interviewed every finalist. Furthermore, there were no standardized questions asked. When the acting board member was not selected, she was understandably bitter about the process and decried the lack of transparency and fairness. This board continued to feel the impact of that mismanaged process for several years, until all of the parties had departed.

A consultant who works with many nonprofits said that she rarely sees organizations that do performance evaluations. She further noted the difficulty this creates. If employees—particularly executive directors or clergy—are performing well, their morale sinks if they are never told that they're doing a good job. If performance deteriorates, those having difficult conversations are forced to backtrack and reference behaviors that have perhaps been forgotten. Any opportunity for productive change has been lost.

A mid-sized nonprofit lost their founding executive director and opened a nation-wide search. The board anticipated, accurately, that the process would require at least six months, because they planned to include an organizational assessment. The problem, which no one wanted to address, was the dysfunction of the remaining staff. Over the years of the former executive director's tenure, there had been widespread staff unhappiness and turnover. In an effort to keep the programs and projects moving, remaining staff were shifted from position to position, and new people were hired with little thought. Consequently, the organization lost all track of what positions would best serve the organization. They were fairly certain that employees were not assigned to areas where their skills served them or the organization well. The board averted several near-crises in financial mismanagement and staff/board conflict as they focused exclusively on the selection of executive director. Fortunately, their careful search for the executive director provided a strong leader able to manage staff and realign positions.

Jim Collins, when talking about great companies and their approach to people, famously paraphrased the leaders whom he interviewed. "If we get the right people on the bus, the right people in the right seats, and the wrong people off the bus, then we'll figure out how to take it someplace great."3 The "bus" for every nonprofit is populated by the board and the staff. They can steer the organization in the right direction, avoiding the crisis potholes, or they can become the distractions that cause a calamity. It is important that the process of selecting and managing both board and staff be undertaken with a strategic vision, with appropriate professional skills for hiring and managing. When people do not fit the organization's goals, they must be dismissed. Good boards and good staff do not just happen; they are created with intensive time, energy, and focus.

PRECURSORS TO CRISES

It is important to be able to identify a crisis *when one occurs, in order to employ the tools and levels of response to effectively limit damage. It is also important to be able to distinguish which problems encountered in the daily management of a nonprofit organization might, if unchecked, lead to a crisis. Conflict that is not addressed or does not abate—whether within the office, within the board, or with other constituencies—can grow to unmanageable proportions. There are other issues which may also be precursors to crisis in the realm of policy violations or personnel offenses. Wise leaders learn to intervene sooner rather than later.*

CHAPTER 4

Somewhere between a full-blown crisis and the aspirin-inducing pains of day-to-day management is the gray landscape of events which might or might not foreshadow a crisis. These are the more-than-just-annoying situations which, if not addressed, can lead to catastrophes. There are ways to differentiate which problems should attract a leader's attention.

Measuring Severity

- It is vital to know whether a problem is *acute* or *chronic*. That understanding determines what solutions might be sought. If this is a conflict about a specific decision or event, it is probably something that can be addressed with reasonable problem-solving by reasonable, problem-solving people. If this is a behavior precipitated by something out of the ordinary, a flexible response is appropriate; if it reflects consistent disregard for procedures, corrective action is called for. If it involves a general morass of bad feelings or unhappy relationships, teasing out a solution may be more difficult. The more difficult things are to resolve, the more likely they are to continue. Tensions that continue seldom improve. If the problem has been going on for a few weeks, then it is something worthy of concern—not panic, but concern. If it has been going on for a month, it is an issue that is becoming resistant to resolution.

- It is important to consider whether *resolution has been attempted*. If no one has addressed the situation, then a legitimate question is, "Why not?" If it is simply that things got out of hand, and it took a while to realize that there was a problem, then a leader is positioned to try to bring some resolution. If the answer is something else—that people who could address the problem are part of the problem; that no one knows what to do or say; that some are afraid of the people who are creating the conflict; that no one understands why people are unhappy or angry, and they don't know how to make things better; or that some think this is not a real issue—then the problem focus begins to emerge.

If someone *has* tried to address the problem, the question then becomes: who intervened and how directly? Is it possible that the message was not received or was misunderstood? If a reasonable attempt was made by someone in authority to resolve the conflict and, yet, tensions remain, this raises the level of risk that the situation might become a full crisis. If there is no one to intervene, for whatever reason, this also raises the level of risk.

- A part of the assessment of problems is gauging whether the tension or conflict is *escalating*. Are more people getting drawn in? Did a dispute which involved two people become "sides" involving many people? Are the times of silence, tension, or fighting becoming more frequent or intense? If so, this is moving toward a crisis.

- The seriousness is also calculated by whether this is an *internal or an external issue*. If the dispute is confined to those who work for the nonprofit or church, i.e., the staff or board, leaders have more authority and ability to address the issues and hopefully resolve differences amicably. If the issue involves those peripheral to the organization, like volunteers (although they may be both internal and external in many nonprofits), donors, clients, or community people, then this raises the level of risk. The risk is especially high when the escalation of tension has led to a conflict moving outside the walls from where it began, i.e., outside the board room or staff offices.

Assessing Tools Already in Place

As with the analysis of a full blown crisis, assessment of the seriousness of a pre-crisis will cause a leader to re-examine policies and people.

1. Are there policies in place that might address the questions being bandied about?

2. If there are no policies currently on the books, what might a new policy look like? If a policy were to be introduced to this situation as a future resolution, what might be the response of those who are in conflict?

3. Are there policies that have not been enforced, or have been enforced erratically, that may have created confusion or conflict?

4. Are the roles clear for the people who are involved in the situation? If not, why not? Is that lack of clarity something that could be addressed to good effect?

5. Are there disciplinary issues for any of the people involved which have been addressed previously? Were these recorded? Were all parties clear about the implications of the disciplinary conversation?

6. If the disciplinary issues were not addressed, why not? Is this something that can be done now, in this situation?

7. Are there concrete decisions or physical realities that need to be considered or reconsidered, such as heat, cold, safety, or hours of work?

8. What is the role of the board? Are they aware of the problem? Are they part of the problem?

9. What is the organization's process for resolving difficulties? Is there a personnel committee of the board? Is there a place for staff to lodge complaints? Is there an appeal process? Is there a built-in requirement to invoke mediation? Is there a whistle-blower policy and is this relevant?

10. Are there answers to questions which could be provided by outside resources, such as the insurance company, auditor, or the organization's attorney?

11. Have any violations of internal or external policy or law been revealed?

It is human nature to want to ignore problems. Most people hope others will resolve their own issues or take hints or be satisfied with the answers or solutions provided. Sometimes, leaders are slow to realize that things are moving down the wrong track—and perhaps moving rapidly and with disastrous consequences. Even without the questions raised in this chapter, good leaders usually know or sense when there are problems which need to be addressed. It is so much easier to address these situations at the early stage, rather than letting them become true, full-blown conflicts, much less full-blown crises.

Acknowledging and Managing Conflict

Somewhere between prevention and cure, in the arena of crises, is conflict management. There is nothing wrong with disagreements or even conflict. It is the unresolved disagreement that escalates conflict and becomes disruptive for everyone. It is important to recognize that prolonged conflict is uncomfortable for everyone, including those who are not directly involved. Most people can think of situations when, as an inadvertent observer to a quarrel—whether on the street, in a store, or in the circle of family or friends—the discomfort was severe. It is embarrassing and disconcerting to be in the middle of conflict. Knowing that, a leader must prevent conflict from getting a foothold in an organization.

No one likes to deal with conflict. As someone who has been actively involved with resolving disputes and managing conflict for the past twenty-five years, I admit that I never go into a situation as a mediator or conflict manager without some fear and trepidation. In part, it is the unpredictability of conflict. We fear doing the wrong thing and making things worse. We worry about loss of control—our own self-control or that of others. As a professional mediator, I worry that I will assert too much authority over the process and not allow for a free flow of concerns and potential solutions.

Unrecognized or unmanaged conflict can definitely lead to bad things happening in organizations. A secondary effect of conflict can become a crisis, simply because conflict distracts people from the things they should focus on. Conflict can lead to inattention to safety regulations, missed deadlines, or rude treatment of clients. Learning to recognize conflict and engage it, productively and perhaps proactively, is a valuable tool for the prevention of crises.

Timing and Time

Mediation, conflict management, and dispute resolution are the subjects of degree and certificate programs; they are the specialties of respected professions and are part of sub-specialties in other professions like law. Nothing in a short book about crises will prepare average boards or leaders to handle situations with the competence of those who have been trained. But it is possible to manage conflict effectively in its early stages and prevent crises. Indeed, most professional managers of crises state that by the time they are called into situations, productive work or resolution of grievances is often impossible. The earlier that intervention can be introduced, the more likely the success of the process and a positive outcome.

Sometimes, the reason people don't do the right thing is that they are hurrying to do things right. In the late nineties, I was part of a team that was privileged to work with the Jamaican Constabulary Force, training officers and patrolmen in mediation skills. In the first session with the police, several experienced men expressed concern about the time it would take to mediate in the midst of potentially explosive situations on the street. To try to "talk things out" sounded blatantly ridiculous to some. When we asked about their normal procedures for arrest and confinement of disputants, it became clear that the process was quite time-consuming. At the end of weeks of training and role-playing, the officers and patrolmen became convinced that mediation was not only an effective tool, but was also a more efficient use of their time and skills than their previous methods. Some nonprofit leaders may be concerned about a conflict management process being too cumbersome. When weighed against the nagging buzz of low grade discord and occasional outbursts of hostility, it seems likely that directly confronting these issues and people would be more effective and efficient.

Two Key Responses to Conflicts

There are two simple things to remember about those who are engaged in conflict:

➢ Most people want to be heard.

➢ Often, people simply want someone to say they're sorry.

In theory, those are simple things that should be easy enough to offer—thus ending 75 percent of all conflicts and short-circuiting many crises. But apparently it is not that easy for people to really listen to others or to apologize. It is especially difficult to do with authenticity. *Listening for comprehension* is what one consultant called this skill. Many of the pre-crises which have turned into crises could have been resolved by offering either or both of these two remedies.

People usually want to solve conflicts, but they aren't sure how to go about it. In her book *How to Reduce Workplace Conflict and Stress,* Anna Maravelas writes, "When work groups are presented with a route toward resolution, and a mere outline of a competent process, they pull together, suspend self-oriented needs, and arrive at our meetings with renewed optimism, and with their sleeves rolled up, ready to work and begin anew. Individuals want to be connected ... The motivation exists. We need only provide the opportunity for its expression."4

Conflict Management 101

In any situation, anyone can be a peacemaker by using the following steps to address conflict. It helps if that person has the authority of his or her office, like a board or council president or executive director. But anyone can assert a voice of reason, play a neutral role, and reduce tensions.

- Recognize there is a problem. While leaders often have a fear of intervening precipitously, that is probably a smaller risk than the alternative. If people genuinely don't have an issue, they will be helped by knowing that there are others to whom it *appears* they have a conflict. If they do have an issue but deny it, they will likewise realize it is affecting the group. In any case, the person who first identified the conflict encourages resolution so that everyone can move on to other matters.

- Create an opportunity for neutral discussion of the issue. This does *not* mean in the middle of a meeting, in one of the parties' offices, at a particularly busy time, or in a public place like a restaurant. Ask the two (or more) individuals if they would be willing to talk more about things, offering a neutral place to meet and a choice of times. Frame the meeting as a time for all of you to listen to each other and brainstorm some solutions that would allow all parties to continue working effectively together.

- When meeting, set some ground rules and lay out the parameters: "Can we agree that we will talk for no more than an hour and see where we are? I would like to serve as the neutral party here, making sure we stay on track. It goes without saying we will not interrupt, etc." The leader's role is to manage the process of conflict resolution but not the outcome. Frame the issue and articulate the potential for positive outcomes. The leader can encourage people to listen well, speak reasonably, and come up with realistic solutions. Make it clear from the beginning that each participant will have opportunities to talk; each will have opportunities to listen; each will have opportunities to make suggestions for resolution of the problem that concerns them. Get a commitment to confidentiality from all parties.

- Allow each person the opportunity to describe his or her view of things, uninterrupted.

- The neutral party must also listen, encourage the parties not speaking to listen, and summarize what is said in neutral language without editorializing. Do this for each person. Try to equalize the amount of time each spends speaking.

- Summarize the issues, noting places where they agree. ("You both are committed to the organization and want things to go well," or "You are both frustrated by the toll taken by this conflict and would like to resolve things and move on," etc.

- Ask for suggestions for how to move forward. Listen to the suggestions and ask questions to get specificity. ("What would that mean, exactly?") Find points of agreement. Summarize. Check back with the other persons to see what they think of the suggestions.

- Ask for an agreement—in writing or verbally. Try to identify any places of ambiguity. Express confidence that this can work (if, in fact, you think it can).5

If a clear conflict exists and there is no one willing and able to address the situation, consider hiring an outside mediator. Most communities have mediation centers or groups that offer mediation services. They protect the confidentiality of the organization and are truly neutral parties with professional skills and broad experience.

Notes to the neutral party:

- Don't get focused on who is telling the truth. It doesn't matter. You are not a judge. What matters is coming up with a solution or solutions to get past this and prevent a real crisis.

- Carefully manage the process and the parties so there can be some resolution. Assume that people have good intentions and want to be free of the conflict.

- Don't force an agreement. If there isn't any resolution possible, then express appreciation for their effort, express concern about the impact their continued conflict is having on others, and suggest that they might want to meet again with each other or with you or with someone else.

- Be a non-anxious presence. Anxiety is contagious, but so is calm. Conflict makes everyone anxious—especially the participants. Having someone who speaks in a calm, matter-of-fact way makes others relax and enables everyone to think ahead to conflict resolution.

- If the very thought of going through this process with the people in conflict terrifies you, find a friend with whom you can role play. It feels silly, but it will help you feel more comfortable in the situation

Unresolved conflict is not only the most common complaint heard in the nonprofit halls, it is also the issue most likely to slip under the radar and be ignored by leaders.

While unresolved conflict is dangerous, it is not the only precursor to crisis. Other red flags, such as disregard for policies and serious personnel issues, are harbingers of more critical problems. They are warnings that leaders should pay further attention to such situations in order to forestall a crisis.

Bullies

There's a component of conflict about which there has been little written for the nonprofit workplace—dealing with bullies. There are resources online that help people deal with bullies in the business workplace and, of course, in schools. But the impact of bullies in a small nonprofit organization is magnified. It is not uncommon to encounter bullies when working with nonprofits, where they tend to surface in positions of responsibility. In the business environment, there is usually a Human Resources department or a supervisor that can be contacted, even if it is a manager accused of misbehaving. Bullies thrive in an atmosphere of loose authority, amid mild-mannered people who just want to do the right thing. Too often this describes nonprofit organizations. Pastors have bullied their congregations; executive directors have threatened boards, saying they would leave or sue; board presidents have dared other board members to object to anything they say or do.

Bullying is different from harassment or even aggression. According to the Department of Labor and Industries, "workplace bullying refers to repeated unreasonable actions of individuals (or a group) directed toward an employee or a group of employees which is intended to intimidate and creates a risk to the health and safety of the employee. Workplace bullying often involves an abuse or misuse of power. Bullying includes behavior that intimidates, degrades, offends, or humiliates a worker, often in front of others." It is important to identify whether or not an organization has this issue for several practical reasons:

- Bullying costs organizations money due to absences, grievances, and failure to meet organizational goals.

- Bullying may call forth legal actions.

- Bullying leads to crises. In the words of the same document from the DLI, "Bullies do not run good organizations ... the breakdown of trust in a bullying environment may mean employees will fail to contribute their best work, do not give extra ideas for improvement, do not provide feedback on failures and may be less honest about performance."

Bullies cannot be handled in the way that one might otherwise address conflicts or troublesome people. They are in a different category. Why?

- Bullies thrive on conflict. Whereas most people would like to avoid confrontations, bullies enjoy the power of making others uncomfortable. When leaders are conflict-averse, bullies take over.

- Bullies are unable or unwilling to take hints. Often direct requests to cease conversations or behaviors are ignored.

- Like other types of abusers, they are very good at blaming others. Their blame is usually public, loud, and embarrassing to others who may shy away from the display.

- Bullies may alternate negative behaviors with being useful or supportive, so that when called out for abusive reactions, they can respond with all that they have done for the organization lately.

- People are afraid to disagree with bullies, thus reinforcing their power, and increasing the incidents of bullying.

When there is a true bully in the organization, this person needs to be dealt with quickly. When handling a workplace bully, the goal is to act fast to show that the organization won't tolerate bad behavior. The biggest mistake employers make, according to Gary Namie of the Workplace Bullying Institute, is that they don't pay attention to bullying until it results in a crisis. Dealing with a bully who is a board or council president or even executive director is more difficult than when the bully is a middle manager or employee.

Here are hints from the several studies that have been done:

- When confronting, be matter-of-fact and not confrontational or emotional.

- Be specific about the behavior, make statements such as, "You shouted at the board secretary," or "You called Joe an idiot."

- Target the behavior and not the person. Do not ask the person to "change;" tell the bully the behavior must stop.

- Document the behavior, the conversation with the person, and any consequences that are defined.

- Quantify the number of complaints and the time spent dealing with complaints.

- Bullies can be incorporated into a formal process of mediation, but only if their bullying is controlled by ground rules, and they are urged to contribute to resolutions.

- Sometimes addressing the bully both publicly and privately is more effective than only talking one-on-one.

The longer bullying goes on, the more difficult it is to control or stop. Especially in nonprofits, the responsibility for ensuring a healthy work environment must fall to everyone. Ignoring bad behavior makes it likely the incivility will spread.6

Many people are appalled at the idea that serious conflict or bullying could exist in faith-based or nonprofit organizations. It may be unrealistic, but nonprofits are held to a higher level of expectation. This is all the more reason to be vigilant in modeling healthy workplace relationships. It is surprising, the number of nonprofit workplaces that have allowed bullying to become a part of the culture. And it creates a dangerous path to a crisis.

Examples of Precursors to Crises

A colleague had been a very effective and productive executive director of a community nonprofit for more than ten years. One year she found herself working with a husband-and-wife team as board members. The wife had been an important part of board work and a good team member for the previous two years. The husband was a professional in a field where the board needed expertise. My friend confessed later that she had a twinge of concern when the spouse was voted on, but hoped her nervousness was unfounded. Sadly, the spouse was argumentative and negative and the tone of board meetings changed. Eventually, the executive director wisely asked for a meeting with the new board member. She had thought things through well and described to him what she was observing in his interactions. She asked if he was happy being on the board. He confessed he was not. It was a productive meeting in which they reached a mutual agreement that he would resign. This was great conflict resolution, preventing what might have been a crisis in the form of massive board exits or an inability to focus on the work the board needed to do.

A church decided to sell its adjoining land to another nonprofit in the community. Both organizations were part of larger national groups. Several in the church objected to the mission of the nonprofit that was going to purchase the property. They brought their concerns to the council, but there were prevailing financial concerns and the council decided to proceed. The disgruntled group went to others outside the church who agreed with their political/social concerns, and the situation escalated so quickly that there were soon protests, electronic and actual, in that community and across the country. The speed of Internet communication allows concerns to be quickly and broadly shared. The focused passion of a few people, which might have been balanced by a commitment to the organization—or, in this case, the church—may not be so moderated among those who view things from a distance. The church backed out of its agreement, but the damage was done. What had been a single incident became a conflict, which became a crisis, which threatened the church's existence. It was a full year before any normalcy was achieved, and, by then, many people had left the congregation and dollars had been drastically reduced, causing programs to die and more families to leave.

A client of a social service organization felt she had been ignored by the staff person assigned to work with her. She attempted to tell the staff person. She called the director of the agency, but she was told she needed to continue to work with the staff. The client, feeling the situation was unfair and that her child was being endangered, wrote a letter to the newspaper. A local columnist picked up the issue and wrote six consecutive weeks of columns about the organization. The columns began with the situation identified by the client. But when the director wrote an angry letter to the newspaper, defending the organization, the columnist took it upon herself to write scathing articles that noted the relatively high salary of the executive director, the nature of relationships between the board of directors and local businesses, etc. Eventually the board president set up a meeting with the client and other groups in the community. But great damage had been done. The organization listened to people and offered an apology, but it was too late to avoid a crisis.

Financial crises—especially financial mismanagement or theft—almost always begin with small forays into questionable activities. Most could and should have been stopped before they became crises. I know of one financial administrator for a nonprofit who advocates for "healthy paranoia." Having come from the business world, he bemoans the fact that in nonprofits "we like to trust people; we want people to like us." Standard practices in the business world, in terms of applying policies to all, are seen as "insulting" in the nonprofit world. "We're blinded," he says, "by the fuzzy feeling that we're all good-hearted people who care about [families/ animals/ community, etc.]" Consequently, he had observed abuses that led to crises because of the way nonprofits dealt with money matters.

A large and respected nonprofit described a near crisis that involved a key employee. The organization struggled to find a way to deal with this person's abusive, bullying behaviors for seven months, because some of the leadership believed strongly in the possibility of personal change. They were determined to make a good faith effort to mold this employee's behavior into something that would fit the organizational culture. Looking back, they describe this period as nearly devastating to the entire organization, and they now ask themselves, "How did we survive that?" They spent untold amounts of time and money on this one employee, investigating charges made against him and by him; they hired a coach; they developed improvement plans. As their leader noted, if only they had devoted those resources to the cherished employees who functioned well, they would have made such progress. Because the organization now sees the person as poisonous, his behaviors as well beyond difficult and fitting the definition of harassment, they understand why their well-intentioned methods of personnel management failed. There was relief when this person left under pressure along with a certain sense of validation when he was fired quickly from his next position.

Allowing a conflict to continue unabated makes others uneasy at best and highly anxious at worst. Additionally, unresolved conflict escalates tensions and sometimes highlights other issues that can become a breeding ground for a real crisis.

IT'S A CRISIS

When something happens *and leaders are unsure of the event's gravity, it may be helpful to review the checklist from the first chapter. A crisis requires a different and higher level of thinking and acting. This chapter advocates for the board's formal planning for a crisis, to facilitate the enactment of the organization's own emergency plan. While the sample plan can be picked up and utilized without having done the background work, it will be much more effective if the topic of crisis management has been discussed prior to a catastrophe.*

CHAPTER 5

Elements of a Crisis

The elements of a crisis are clear, making it different from simply a concern or a conflict. The important distinctions are found in the answers to these questions.

- Is this something the press might be interested in? This is not just a question of whether or not reporters are currently probing or waiting outside the door. If the media received a call telling them about a situation, might they see it as an interesting story?

- Does the situation involve money? Sex? Endangerment of a child? It's not that those are the only elements of a crisis, but they are definitely hot-button issues. They attract attention and passion.

For a nonprofit to be seen as mishandling money is much more dangerous than for a business to have a money problem. Nonprofits can be accused of embezzlement—or even just the mismanagement of a relatively small amount of money—and this will be seen as a news story. Organizations have been brought down because of allegations that designated funds were not spent on the projects for which the money was donated. Nonprofits depend upon contributions from individuals, corporations, foundations, and public entities. They must always be seen as careful with what they spend and meticulous in their accounting.

Sex attracts attention, no matter what the context or content. Put sex together with a nonprofit or church and it is a scandal—even if nothing can be proved. If there are allegations of sexual wrongdoing attached to a nonprofit, then that agency or church has a crisis. There was a newspaper story about a volunteer who was found to be on the sex-offender list for a crime committed more than a decade earlier, involving a sixteen-year-old girl, when the volunteer was twenty. This became a serious threat to the organization.

If a child is endangered or hurt, and the injury or death is attached to the organization, it is a crisis. Public perception is such that children must be protected by adults at all cost.

- Is this a potential lawsuit, with the organization as either plaintiff or defendant? In this day and age, almost every situation must be regarded as such. Flood? Fire? Yes, even when there is no loss of life. Anything involving death or injury is definitely a potential lawsuit. Firings or internal office disputes must be regarded as potentially legal issues. Further, if the organization knows it is going to be sued, no matter how frivolous or wrongfully-portrayed leaders perceive it to be, they must assume this is a crisis. It may attract the attention of the press; it will require resources and attention until it is disposed of; it may impact the ability to pursue the mission of the organization. In other words, this issue may cause leaders to own many other problems mentioned in this list.

- Does the situation threaten the organization's credibility? This is a complex question. An employee or board member may not feel that this issue impairs the organization's integrity. But it must be evaluated from the standpoint of others who know very little about the inner workings of the program or office. The media and the words spoken by others in the community cannot be controlled. A group's credibility is dependent on the level of trust built over years of service. Will this situation undermine that trust?

- Does this situation threaten the organization's very existence? Many aspects of a calamity can do that: the destruction of a building; the mass exodus of people; the loss of funding or amassing of debt; the complete loss of credibility noted above.

There are many sources of information on the Internet and in print that give advice to businesses for handling crises. They are worth reading. But there are differences in how a business and how a nonprofit organization are impacted by a crisis and, therefore, in how they deal with a catastrophe. These differences are more significant than just the size of most large businesses or corporations. Thinking of the original test for what constitutes a crisis, the only thing that might threaten the existence of a *company* would be its profit-making services or products. The Tylenol tampering crisis in the eighties almost brought down Johnson & Johnson and caused major changes in how the company packaged its products. (Unfortunately, the company has reentered the same waters with questions of product safety). The Toyota safety problems created a crisis for the automobile company. Nonprofits don't have a product to sell. Their credibility, their integrity, is what allows them to retain the community support on which they depend—in dollars, volunteers, and clients. A crisis for a nonprofit is far more serious and less easily dismissed than problems that befall businesses.

An Identified Crisis is the Reality

Perhaps a nonprofit has correctly done everything possible. The policies and people are in place. And still a crisis occurs. Or, more likely, everything wasn't done perfectly, but the organization proceeded with commitment and passion, doing the best job possible.

A crisis can never be treated casually. If a reporter calls in the middle of the night to say there has been a break-in at the office, and the executive director arrives to be greeted by a television crew, whoever responds to the call must try to offer only information of which they are certain, with a focus on continuing the organization's mission, and with the caveat that leadership will assess the situation. But it is helpful to have thought about this kind of scenario before it occurs in the middle of the night.

Every office has a safety plan to exit the building in case of fire or other endangerments. These plans are periodically revisited and rehearsed. Organizations have other safety regulations involving procedures to follow if a worker becomes ill, etc. The plans are often laminated and posted in highly visible places. Think of emergency planning as a way to protect the life of the organization. What follows is a sample outline for an emergency plan that every organization can adapt. To customize the plan for an organization will require the gathering of a complete inventory of vital information. This is detailed in the Crisis Contingency Plan in Chapter Seven. That exercise will provide the board with important information, even if a disaster never strikes. An emergency plan is in the same category as personal estate planning, wills, and succession planning. It is uncomfortable to anticipate disasters or death. It evokes a sense of almost superstitious fear that we are inviting the very thing we dread. But having a plan and then implementing important conversations that lead to comprehensive data gathering will create a sense of confidence. Should a calamity strike, the organization will be able to respond efficiently and effectively, and the public will know that thoughtful leaders were in charge.

Emergency Plan in Time of Crisis

When an organization is in the midst of a crisis, this is the emergency plan that must be followed:

- **Notify the board or council**. They should meet as quickly as possible. To repeat, they are legally and fiscally responsible for the nonprofit.

- **Define and clarify confidentiality**. It is not unreasonable to ask individuals for a commitment to confidentiality. It is that important. Depending upon the situation, the size of the community, and the media market, discretion may be what protects the credibility of the organization.

- **Gather information** so the managing group can be briefed on the situation. A board must be able to ask questions freely and raise any and all concerns. A good leader will create a climate of helpful questioning and brainstorming that minimizes defensiveness and encourages candor. More information will come in over time. But, for this initial meeting, *all* information is important.

- **Discuss who will act as the spokesperson** to represent the organization during the situation. Ideally, there is a policy regarding communication, but, if not, the board must identify who is to speak on behalf of the church or nonprofit, with the additional specification that no one else can or will speak publicly. Usually, this is the board president or church council president and not a paid employee. But it is important to take into consideration how comfortable and capable each person is when speaking to the press. For some, this type of public communication is simply unmanageable. Answering press questions is delicate and requires knowledge of potential liability, careful use of language, self-confidence, a grasp of the organization's mission, and sensitivity to protecting the privacy of staff, clients, and others.

- **Prepare a press statement** approved by the board, even if it is thought not to be necessary. Perhaps the group will want to release the statement in order to frame the crisis in their own words. This statement may need to be crafted by a communications professional or looked over by an attorney before your board gives final approval.

- **Strategize** how the organization will approach the crisis within the rest of the community, both constituents and the public at large.

- **Determine the support of other professionals** that might be needed—accountants, attorneys, building contractors, etc. Occasionally a situation is so egregious that a group might be advised to hire someone to act as the organization's spokesperson. In this day and age, it is a rare situation that does not require the help and advice of an attorney. It is best to always assume that a crisis may result in a lawsuit, either something the organization defends against or initiates. This is true whether the crisis is part of a natural disaster or impacted by humans.

- **Gather information about the two elements which were points of prevention: policies and people.** What policies are relevant to this crisis? If there was a specific policy, was it implemented? This may be part of press statements and/or talking points. If there was no policy, per se, was the staff still alert to the areas that created the crisis? For example, if the organization seems to have been the victim of a theft, is it policy to have an annual audit? If not, is there an annual reconciliation of accounts? Who does this, and when was it last done? If the crisis was a physical accident, what is policy concerning safety? Are there trainings regarding safety? If the organization suffered from a hurricane, are there policies regarding hurricanes? These pieces of information will be important to know.

- **Explore all information about any personnel** who might have been involved and the history of their work with the nonprofit. How were they selected? Were background checks conducted when they were hired? Were references contacted? How long were they employed? What training was offered or required? Was anyone on the staff trained, for example, in CPR? The information derived about individuals may not be appropriate to share with the public, but it might be appropriate and helpful to the organization.

- **Estimate how long the crisis will require attention and create an appropriate plan.** What are the elements of this situation that must be addressed in the weeks or months ahead? If a natural disaster has occurred, there will be physical clean-up to be done. Sometimes human situations require clean-up. Who will be responsible for each task? Differentiate between which assignments should be completed by staff, the board, or outside persons. While this varies according to the size of the organization, it is important to create accountability and avoid duplication of effort. List tasks and assign names.

- **Create an ongoing communication plan**. While the press may need to be dealt with in an on-going way, others also require tending. Internal people—staff and volunteers—will need communication about what has happened, what is planned, what is expected. External partners will also need communication—donors, community partners, fellow nonprofits or churches, neighbors, and organizational headquarters.

- **Develop talking points** with basic information included. If the office has a receptionist, or if volunteers or others answer the telephones, each person should have a simple statement which can be offered when questions are asked from outside the organization. There should be no deviation from the script, and people should be trained about how to handle questions. It may be important to keep a log of people who call, who took the call, and what responses were given. Consider the organization's website and social media as ways to communicate carefully constructed messages.

- **Borrow from the experiences or experts of other organizations**. Usually there is another nonprofit which has been through a similar challenge. What advice might come from them or from a parent organization? Do they have experts (legal, communication) who can provide support and/or consultation?

- **Consider the advice of communication professionals to get out ahead of a negative story**. Initially, giving little information is not only a good idea but can prevent dangerous misunderstandings. However, the minimalist, lock-down approach cannot continue. The organization may begin to lose credibility simply because they are not seen as honest or forthright. Analyzing the crisis from a public relations perspective can help the organization manage elements of the situation which might be cast in a negative light if revealed initially by others. There is a difference between a story that reads, "Employee of Mayberry Art League is arrested for embezzlement of $5,000 in membership fees" and one that reads, "Audits by the board of the Mayberry Art League revealed a discrepancy in funds that have resulted in organizational changes."

- **Make no assumptions about the media.** They are not the enemy, out to trick the agency or present incidents in a negative light. But neither are they a friend, regardless of how many positive stories they may have offered about the organization in the past. You should never think that anything said will not be reported, no matter what the caveats. Reporters are another professional entity. They are doing their jobs and trying to get a story. You can, however, build a mutually supportive relationship by giving factual information to reporters, trying to understand and meet their internal deadlines, and articulating the overall mission of your organization so it can be understood by the public as the crucial context for the story.

These are the elements of the Emergency Plan. When needed, they can be modified and can guide the organization through what might otherwise be a chaotic period. The final chapter defines the pre-work that responsible boards should undertake to develop a more complete and specialized emergency plan if calamity strikes. The Crisis Contingency Plan can and should be worked out by the board when no hint of a crisis is on the horizon. The plan includes the creation of a Crisis Audit Team to act as an annual sentry to protect the nonprofit organization. The appendix lays out a manageable six-month board plan to gather the necessary information and implement key policies.

Examples of Crisis Management

An organization was the victim of a large embezzlement. Dealing with this crime meant interacting with the police, the district attorney, the press, donors, the head office of the organization, staff, clients, etc. The board immediately determined that they would need additional resources and a budget to pay for their representatives. This was, indeed, a situation that might have destroyed the organization. Their plan included seeking a loan to cover the immediate expenses they thought they might incur; appointing a board spokesperson; contacting the firm that did their last audit; contacting an attorney;

contracting pro bono public relations services; speaking with staff and volunteers in order to silence any public or premature gossip about the circumstances and person involved; and contacting key donors and volunteers to ask for their support. A year after this very public and embarrassing incident, the organization was not just functioning but flourishing.

As a new executive director, I was in my office when I received a call that a serious accident had taken place on site. Several volunteers had been injured and were being taken to the hospital by emergency vehicles. We had no organizational plan, so every action was undertaken with fear and adrenaline, which soon gave way to fatigue. I called the board president. I met the ambulance; I stayed at the hospital; I contacted relatives to inform them of the injuries and to give them contact information; I spoke with those on site who were not victims, to reassure them. Then I met with the board of directors, an attorney, and our own staff who were present. Finally, as an organization, we regrouped to see if we had honestly done all we could to prevent this accident and to determine what we might do to ensure that nothing like this would ever happen again. It was painful then and is painful to recall now. We were very fortunate not to have any legal or media actions that might have undermined our ability to move forward.

When the suicide of a board member took place following the discovery and newspaper story of a rather small amount of missing money, the nonprofit did not take any steps. They were paralyzed by the tragedy and could only think personally rather than organizationally. While this is understandable, it is also why this book is written. Being prepared with a public statement, should one be required, can prevent awkward or even libelous statements from being elicited by others, which might compound a difficult situation. Although it was a situation which could have been resolved, and the work of the group could have continued, the nonprofit never did recover.

Two other organizations had relatively small incidents of financial mismanagement on the part of their director. In the first, the organization took all of the protective steps recommended. They determined they needed to put the executive director on leave; then, after doing their due diligence, they fired him. They wrote a brief but specific letter to their supporters saying that their policies and procedures had uncovered some financial irregularities. The board had investigated and had taken steps to ensure that they knew the extent of the damage and that they had stopped any further harm. They apologized for the problem, assured constituents of their ongoing diligence, and asked for their continued support.

In the second organization, the board attempted to hide their discovery from as many people as possible. They fired the executive director and immediately began searching for a new executive director. Because they hadn't really looked at the fabric of the organization or job description, evaluated the pay scale, or interviewed the rest of the staff, they were not in a strong position to hire, much less to turn over a new leaf. They hired quickly with little foresight. Most importantly, they had neither performed a self-assessment nor identified or repaired any of the systemic difficulties that allowed the problem to happen and go undetected in the first place. This began a revolving door of directors which continues to this day.

A fire in a building owned by a nonprofit killed a person squatting in the building, and the organization cooperated fully with the accident investigation. They withheld all public statements that might have presupposed any determination of the cause of the fire or the reason for the death until the investigation was complete. Of course, they expressed their genuine sympathy. When arson was ruled out and the person's death was listed as accidental, they issued appropriate statements about their policies and the most recent building inspection. Their good relations with their neighbors in the community held them in good stead in the face of this crisis. It never became something which threatened the organization.

Because of the controversial nature of its program focus, one nonprofit has experienced multiple crises in the past several years. Initially, the executive director noted that they "had something in place that no one looked at." Now, he said, they have an emergency plan—including a crisis communication plan—and it has added an element of peace of mind to board and staff.

When crises occur, policies (and evidence that those policies were noted and followed) as well as good people have protected many a nonprofit from lawsuits due to public relations disasters, financial crises, contested firings, formal complaints from someone not selected as a client, shootings, sexual harassments, and public board conflict. If policies are known, followed, and recorded, the public will discern care.

If people as a whole—board, staff, and volunteers—reflect well on the organization, the public will be more sympathetic to the fact that illnesses and accidents happen.

THE CRISIS HAS PASSED

After the crisis has passed, *there is still important to work to do. There are relationships to rebuild; trust must be restored. There is the need to assess the crisis from the perspective of hindsight and to determine whether the organization's policies and people were able to stand the test. After lessons are learned, improvements can be made. If this step is skipped, it is almost certain that other crises—whether different from or similar to the first—will follow.*

CHAPTER 6

A critical time in the life of an organization comes *after* it has experienced a crisis. The majority of the repair work has been done, and people are back at their tasks. There is a natural tendency for the board and staff to slump in exhaustion. But this needs to be a time of vigilance. There are very real but usually invisible fissures in an organization or church after a crisis. Regardless of the type of crisis, natural or human-generated, there will almost certainly be left-over emotions. There may be regrets or fears of losing one's job; there may be accusations that couldn't be voiced during the crisis itself; there may be concern that something similar will happen again; and there are often divisions within or between the staff and board. Unless these are brought into the open and addressed, they will resurface later or emerge disguised as other issues and undermine further good work.

Evaluation

An assessment of what contributed to the crisis and how the agency or church responded is an important learning step. The board/council should do this with a focus on improving their crisis management in the future. There is little value in casting blame, but there is great value in identifying things that went well and things that need to be improved upon. Every person who is part of the organization should be allowed input. Indeed, the act of formally processing the crisis after the fact is educational for all concerned. It sends a message, internally and externally, that leadership takes things seriously. While it might seem like a good idea if this sort of assessment were to be done in written form, there are caveats. Honest evaluations that might assume some responsibility for an event should be verbal. Written records should make recommendations. It is unfortunate, but candid assessments that imply wrongdoing may be seen as larger admissions of guilt than they actually are or are intended to be. *Any* written reports must be guarded and kept confidential. If a legal suit is a possibility, the organization's attorney may discourage any written assessments of the situation while things are fluid.

Regardless of written reports, conversations within the board and between the board and staff are certainly a good idea. A thorough review of policies should occur during this phase. Start with a review of the emergency plan utilized. Was it useful in the face of a crisis? What might be modified to create a better response? On the broader front, what policies might be called for in the future? What changes to current policies are called for by this critical event?

Communication

This part of crisis management should also include a follow-up communication plan. The organization will need to reach out to parts of the community to both thank them and to inform them of changes that have been made. The staff, volunteers, donors, and clients will want to understand what changes might take place and why this will bring improvements. There may be physical changes that need to be made—reinforced security; more stringent computer back-ups; new policies or improvements in old policies; or personnel changes. All of these will benefit from careful explanation.

Some of what is discussed in the context of curing a crisis is actually public relations. Public relations is not a frosting of lies to cover up flaws on your organizational cake. A communication strategy is necessary for building or rebuilding trust within the community. The public knows little about what goes on inside the organization. A disaster, even when not preventable, must be followed by a demonstration that care was taken ahead of time to minimize damage. Further, the public wants to know that good policies and good people were in place to deal with problems in responsible ways—and that they continue to remain in place.

Personnel Assessment

A part of correcting any organizational deficiencies after a crisis may involve the discipline or removal of personnel. It is important to be cautious about hiring or firing, during or immediately after a crisis. It may be appropriate to relieve someone of duties, temporarily or permanently. Consulting professionals about the legal and public relations impact of this action would be wise. If the organization decides to take this step, it is important not to view this sort of personnel change as *the* solution. Organizations are systems. In systems, every part is impacted by every other part. Removing an individual is never the whole answer. It may be important for real or even symbolic reasons. But many a church or nonprofit group has been certain that by firing their leader, the group would be able to move in a new trajectory.

Not so. Many a nonprofit has heaved a sigh of relief after an executive director left, only to find that the next person behaved in similar ways. The organization's systems that caused the leader to be hired and kept that person functioning will continue to exist without him or her. A crisis is rarely one person's fault, even when it is a crime committed by an individual. Crises that are not caused by outside forces are almost always perpetuated by an internal—and sometimes invisible—system. Even inadequate response to a crisis by a key person may be only the most visible part of a larger dysfunctional system. And when a new person is hired, he or she will be drawn into the force field left behind. For real change to take place, the entire system must be assessed and addressed.

Firing may be an answer, but it is not the *only* answer.

Critical Conditions for Organizations

There are some crises for which assessments or adjustments will be insufficient to remedy the situation. There are crises in which the organization will be on life support for some time; there will be situations in which nothing can save the nonprofit. Red flags include circumstances where:

- There is no money.

- It will cost more money to repair the damage than the organization has.

- The crisis will be protracted, and it will be difficult or impossible to continue programs during this time, i.e., a long legal battle is anticipated; there is no office space; there has been an exodus of board and/or staff.

Returning to the vehicular metaphor, it is sometimes necessary to park the bus while evaluating the mechanics of the vehicle (policies) and the driver and passengers (people). What changes need to be made to ensure the safety of the vehicle and all who come in contact with it? More organizations should consider the military measure of "standing down." A stand-down, in military parlance, is the temporary stopping of offensive military action. Temporarily shutting down all programming, while a serious measure, may be the most strategic and enlightened response after a crisis.

In some cases, staff must be released. It might be possible to collaborate, in the short term, with other nonprofit organizations, perhaps even sharing staff positions. In the most extreme circumstances, organizations must consider bankruptcy or merger. It should be noted that severe crises with extreme and far-reaching damage tend to attach to organizations that have adopted few of the preventive measures recommended here and to groups where the leadership has been "asleep at the wheel." Signs of trouble may have been ignored until the crisis is out of control and the organization is beyond reclamation.

Examples of Nonprofits in the Aftermath of Crises

In the course of conducting interviews for this book, there were countless fascinating stories of things gone badly wrong and of heroes who had snatched victories from the fires of calamities. One such tale involved a financial management crisis. This fairly large nonprofit was found to be violating its own principles, and indeed the principles of its primary mission, by paying some of its staff less than others. The group had several of the organizational weaknesses that sometimes attach to a founding CEO, including high staff turnover in key positions, such as its chief financial officer. The nonprofit discovered its own problem, following internal complaints.

When the board recognized the extent of the wrongdoing, it hired a public relations firm and determined to disclose all wrongdoing to all of its constituents. They revealed their discovery to the government agencies that had given them money; they paid back everything that they determined was owed to their staff, grantors, etc. An amusing side note was that some funders had no mechanism for receiving the remediation. The organization completely changed their board, hired a new CEO, revised their by-laws, and ensured that they were in complete compliance with internal and external requirements. And their reward for this honorable approach was that the organization maintained its integrity and recovered its financial losses. Today it is highly respected as well as successful.

Many nonprofits have shared examples of their boards disintegrating after a crisis. They held together during the peak time; but then some members left, conflicts surfaced, and focus deteriorated in the aftermath. One executive talked of a different problem. She said, "My board is too trusting. They are not critical enough. No one grills me." She discussed her efforts to encourage the board to ask questions. She said, with some sadness, "If I wanted to mislead them, I could."

When a large organization lost it largest donor, the staff were in shock. They determined that they needed to move in three directions simultaneously. They created a coalition with other organizations that had received money from the same source and developed an advocacy campaign. They created regional teams to determine ways to underwrite the programs they needed to maintain. And they looked at ways to adjust their budget, deciding to ask for a fee for some of their services. They shut down everything that did not have to be continued in the immediate time frame. They changed; they reallocated resources; they kept excellent lines of communication within their own key staff; they created a story around their new approach. It was a challenging time, but, thirteen months later, they described themselves as stronger than ever, with a team of tested and committed leaders.

According to many experts who deal with organizations during and after a crisis, the chief mistake nonprofits make is investing energy and time to cover up what has happened rather than to understand the issues and tighten the ship. A deep assessment of the organization's policies and people is the only real prevention of future problems and cure for the crisis at hand.

MAKING THE ORGANIZATION SAFE

To make things work well, organizations must plan. *It is not sufficient to wish and hope. The job of leaders is to make good things happen. Recognizing the potential for crises and the crippling effect they can have on a nonprofit organization compels leaders to plan for a crisis, just as individuals plan for illnesses, accidents, and death. The effort that goes into the Crisis Contingency Plan will be justified, whether it prevents a disaster, assists an organization in recovery, or contributes to the development of an educated and dedicated team of leaders.*

CHAPTER 7

Bad things happen to good organizations, just as they happen to good people. Even if leaders were somehow able to do everything perfectly, crises would still occur. They happen unexpectedly and unfairly. They threaten the good work that good organizations, run by good people, are doing.

Sometimes it is possible to see the vague outlines of a crisis looming, as when an erratic employee berates a client; or money seems to disappear; or answers to questions are not forthcoming; or a hurricane is predicted. But often there is no way to anticipate a crisis. People have nervous breakdowns, sinkholes appear, people fall, random acts of violence occur.

While leaders can't always prevent crises, they can mitigate the risk and the impact by having good policies and good people in place. Neither of these happens without intentionality.

The Importance of Policies and People

Good *policies* are the key. Anyone with the will and foresight can make certain a board adopts good policies. Policies are designed to outlast people. Good people may come and go, but policies are in place to guide *all* of those within the organization. Policies create a climate of support for the right people, and a place where good people want to be. They create a secure environment for all of the people connected to the organization. They allow for precedent to guide decision-making so that groups don't have to begin anew with every situation or every new person. And policies create smart ways to keep good people and get rid of those who are not.

Jim Collins, author of the well-known books, *Good to Great* and *Built to Last*, is famous for his phrase, "getting the right people on the bus and getting the wrong people off the bus." That is very important. But this book would posit that a first requirement is to create a safety net of policies that are fair, consistent, and transparent in their wording and application. Then the bus is mechanically sound and there are seatbelts installed.

Good *people* must be recruited, selected, trained, and supported. Staff and board members must all be genuinely valued. To replace people is very expensive, in dollars as well as important intangible costs. While we hope good people are attracted to the good organizations with the good policies, they don't just wander in. Getting and keeping good people must be a priority for the organization.

Identifying and Addressing Precursors to Crises

Knowing when an incident, culture, or atmosphere is a precursor to serious conflict or crisis gives leaders the opportunity to intervene. Knowing, as a leader, that you are capable and willing to intervene allows you to encourage creative discourse and productive disagreement, without fearing that it will cross into negativity. Dealing with conflict well and early can turn most situations into something positive. Ignoring conflict is always a potential disaster.

Managing the Emergency

When the call comes in the middle of the night, grab the Emergency Plan which is laid out in Chapter Five and diagrammed in the Prescription section at the back of this book. Adjust it to the circumstances of the situation. Knowing that all of the bases have been identified and assigned creates a comfort for board and staff.

Utilizing the Period After the Crisis

Rather than exhaling and moving back to business as usual, a wise board and staff will understand that there are always parts of the organization's systems that may allow or even encourage a crisis to occur, or can become barriers to handling the crisis as effectively and efficiently as desired. Capitalizing on this time to evaluate will minimize the likelihood of another crisis.

Creating a Crisis Contingency Plan

It is challenging to deal effectively with crises at the time they occur—and immediately afterwards. Therefore, it is a wise investment to do an organizational audit of policies and people ahead of time in order to avoid some of the worst that can befall good organizations. Chapter Five provides an emergency plan for the unexpected calamity. However, wise organizations know that they need a more complete and individualized road map to maintain their vigilance without impairing their day-to-day work. A guide for conducting a Crisis Contingency Plan before it is needed includes these steps:

- Have a strategic board conversation about crises. What are the things that could ruin your organization? Where are the vulnerabilities? What is needed to allow the agency to feel confident in its protective underpinnings?

- Individualize a Crisis Contingency Plan, and be able to shift, when necessary, to an emergency plan like the sample. The board will need to have assessed the two elements in the previous chapters: policies and people.

- What policies can guide the organization through a crisis and its aftermath? List current policies by category. What are the *program* policies? What are the *personnel* policies? What are the *building, financial, safety,* and *data security* policies? What policies are missing? Within policies, are there gaps?

- Who are the people who lead this organization? Begin with the board or council. Know the names, positions, and titles of board members as well as how long they have been in that role. Understand the titles and job descriptions of staff members and the reporting relationships. What trainings are required for staff? Which are optional and which have been attended in the last year?

- What systems are in place to prevent or cure problems? Do leaders have conflict management skills? Are there appeals processes in place? Are the systems understood and effective? Who are your internal first responders in the face of a serious problem? Would they be dependable in a crisis?

- Who would speak on behalf of the organization, if it were to be contacted by the media? If that person is not available, who would be the second option? Is this formalized in a communication plan?

With the above information, it is possible to create a storehouse of critical information for the organization. Information should be updated, and the emergency plan should be reviewed annually.

Developing and Utilizing a Crisis Audit Team

In addition to assessing policies and people, nonprofit boards should authorize a Crisis Audit Team. This group of professionals should be drawn from outside the agency. They would function one day a year. After the organizational work of ensuring sound policies and good people, this team would audit the organization's systems in a formal way, much as the financial auditor audits the organization's books. The Crisis Audit Team might be comprised of the community's actual first responders (fire and police), a technology specialist, an attorney, an accountant, and any other person with expertise in the agency's program area, e.g., day care, construction, health services, etc. This team would function with a board mandate to discover and address any vulnerabilities in the organization and to make recommendations for change. On the day of a crisis audit, the team would look at policies and people in each specific focus area and evaluate how they combine to create the necessary protective shield for preventing crises. This is a manageable safeguard for every nonprofit. The planning and implementation for this Crisis Audit Team will be educational for board and staff alike.

Reaping the Rewards of Crisis Management Work

The struggles of the nonprofit stem from the realities listed in the first chapter: lack of resources in time, staff, and money. Paying attention to crisis prevention may feel like an impossible burden. The daily demands continue for everyone, whether board or staff. But, if people realize the importance of protecting the nonprofit's work and reputation, it is possible to create safeguards in a relatively painless way. At the end of this book, we have laid out a six-month plan for crisis prevention. It relies upon an extra thirty to sixty minutes of attention to specific areas at each monthly board and staff meeting. The educational value alone justifies the investment. It may prevent a crisis from visiting your nonprofit. If an accident does happen, this preparatory effort tells your constituents that you were thoughtful and strategic in your work.

Many organizations have come through crises to the other side—some becoming stronger than when they went in—because they were honest in their assessment and intentional in their remedies.

CRISIS **EMERGENCY PLAN** STEPS

Detailed in Chapter 5, the following steps can be modified
to fit your organization when a crisis hits.

BEFORE ANSWERING ANY QUESTIONS

Pick Up List of Possible Public Statements & Amend to Fit Situation
Keep Mission of Organization at Forefront of Any Public Speaking

AS SOON AS POSSIBLE

Notify Board / Council Chair
Define & Clarify Confidentiality with Staff

AT THE EARLIEST OPPORTUNITY

Gather Information About Relevant (to crisis) Policies & Personnel
Call a Meeting with Board / Council

AT BOARD / COUNCIL MEETING

Review Facts & Confidentiality Policy
Agree / Decide on Spokesperson
Create Appropriate Action Plan
Develop Talking Points
Decide Best Way (if possible) to Get Ahead of Negative Press
Decide What (if any) Other Professional Support Needed
Prepare Press Statement

AFTER BOARD / COUNCIL MEETING

Provide Staff with Talking Points
Seek Relevant Advice from Other Experts or Organizations

Prescriptions
IN CASE OF EMERGENCY

BEFORE LEAVING THE BUILDING OR ANSWERING ANY QUESTIONS

- Pick up a list of possible public statements and amend them according to the circumstances you are in.
- Keep the mission of the organization in the forefront of everything that is said.

IMMEDIATELY

- Contact the board or council chair.
- Contact key staff with instructions regarding who is to receive what information.

AT THE EARLIEST OPPORTUNITY

- Gather information that is immediately available and make notes.

- Check policies that are in place and relevant to the situation.
- Interview any staff who have responsibilities that might be touched by the situation.
- Makes notes of any peripheral factors that might have had an impact on the situation (weather, personnel schedules, interactions with any of those involved over the last several weeks, reports of anything out of the ordinary by anyone).
- Call a meeting of the board/council.

AT THE BOARD OR COUNCIL MEETING

- Review known facts.
- Remind everyone of confidentiality, the communication policy, and what to do if they are contacted by the media (refer them to the identified spokesperson and say nothing).
- Determine whether any other professionals need to be engaged: attorney, CPA, etc.
- Create a first-stage plan for the next several days, prioritizing tasks and identifying persons responsible.
- Prepare press statement and identify circumstances suggesting its distribution.

AFTER THE BOARD MEETING

- Notify parent organizations or headquarters and give

them concise, basic information.

- Notify any colleagues in other nonprofits who might be contacted or affected. Ask if they have experience or expertise to share.

- Be certain staff has been appropriately informed and that they have "talking points" in case of questions directed to them.

USEFUL PHRASES

- We are still gathering information and will study the situation to determine the facts.

- Our mission continues to be…

- XYZ nonprofit has always placed a high priority on [fill in the blank], and we will view this unfortunate situation through that lens.

- We are [distressed, saddened, surprised, other] by this event and are appreciative of the work done by [fill in the blank]. We will continue to work with them as we address this situation.

- I will get back to you when I am able to gather more information.

SIX MONTH PLAN
EMERGENCY CONTINGENCY PLANNING

MONTH 1

Board conversation about crises, with brainstorming about areas of vulnerability and concerns.

Policy ad hoc committee creates and/or updates policies, including bylaws, fiscal controls, conflict of interest & personnel.

MONTH 2

Board discussion to adopt creation of and changes to policies.

Communication ad hoc committee formed & works on communication plan.

MONTH 3

Communications ad hoc committee, augmented by public relations professional, present communication plan & one-page "emergency" protocol. Board discusses & adopts.

Executive Director creates Table of Organization, gathers job descriptions & work plans . Compares job descriptions vs. skill sets.

MONTH 6

Crisis Audit Team ad hoc committee recommends Crisis Audit Team and professionals necessary.

Team mission and focus discussed.

Recipient of report decided, along with timeframe for any recommended changes.

MONTH 5

Board reviews ED report on staff job descriptions vs. skill sets and makes recommendations.

Succession planning ad hoc committee creates organizational succession plan with board approval.

Crisis Audit Team ad hoc committee works on details for annual organizational audit.

MONTH 4

Board reviews board membership, term limits, diversity, etc.

Review of committees and their membership.

Recommendation made for any changes.

Ad hoc succession planning committee looks at staff & board positions for draft succession plan.

Six Month Plan
Emergency Contingency Planning

If you don't have the policies in place that you think you need, and if you have questions about how your nonprofit might handle an emergency, make a commitment to ensure that you will take six months to put policies and people together in a way that will create confidence. Keep these things in mind:

- For each section of this plan, have a different ad hoc committee. This will ensure that you have the correct people acting as consultants and will keep people from getting tired of their tasks. Do not limit yourself to current board members, and do not feel this must be a large group. Three or four of the right people, willing to devote a month or two of time, will be sufficient.

- Each ad hoc committee should have one staff or one board representative. In some cases, it should be the executive director or the board president, but not in all cases.

- Always keep in mind the dual roles of board and staff: the board approves policy, direction, and spending; the staff recommends and implements.

- If there is no strategic plan, the information gathered for the emergency plan will produce excellent background to make that task easier.

- If there is no succession plan, make that the last thing the board undertakes as part of this organizational audit.

- Borrow shamelessly from other organizations, but be sure to adapt to your own needs. The best materials to borrow are from organizations of similar size and program focus to your own.

- The very last item is to create and strategize the use of a Crisis Audit Team. Identify the people and processes that allow them to "patrol" the key parts of the organization and recommend improvements that might prevent crises.

Month One

The board has a conversation about crisis, brainstorming areas of vulnerability and identifying concerns.

The policy ad hoc committee begins to gather all policies and procedures that the nonprofit already has in place. Over the next month, this group identifies which policies are being utilized and which are outdated. They also gather two samples of each new policy to be created, with the help of the internet and other organizations. At this stage, the organization will want, at a minimum:

- By-laws
- Fiscal controls policy
- Conflict of interest Policy
- Personnel policy

The committee makes recommendations for policy changes at next month's meeting.

Month Two

The board discusses the policies. It votes to adopt the needed changes and new policies. The board may want to make a policy regarding the availability and use of policies within the organization.

The ad hoc Communication Committee is formed and begins its work.

Month Three

The ad hoc Communications Committee, augmented by a public relations professional, presents a communication plan, complete with a one-page "emergency" protocol. The board discusses and adopts.

The board continues its discussion of policies. Staff members are educated about any ramifications of new policies for their work.

The board authorizes the executive director to create a Table of Organization and gather job descriptions and work plans. The executive director looks for areas of duplicated effort as well as tasks that are not being addressed. The ED also reviews the personnel records of staff to see if personnel are well-matched to their job descriptions.

A separate board committee reviews the board positions and board committees to report in month four.

Month Four

The board chair presents an assessment of board membership, noting length of time served and roles outside the organization's board. A graph will note the diversity of the board in terms of age, gender, professions, race, and geography. The list of committees and their membership is identified. Board committee makes recommendations to the board.

A succession planning committee will begin to work with the group, looking at staff positions as well as board positions, and develop a draft succession plan.

Month Five

The board assesses the "people" component of the organization, focusing on the staff report. The board discusses and reviews the fit of these two groups. The board makes recommendations based upon this information. A succession planning committee inserts data collected into an organizational succession plan. The board approves the succession plan.

The Crisis Audit Team ad hoc committee begins work on details for an annual organizational audit.

Month Six

The Crisis Audit Team Committee recommends a Crisis Audit Team, identifying what positions would be needed for this group. They recommend a specific audit day. The recommendation will include the overall mission of the team and the focus of each member of the team. The plan will specify who will receive the report and the time frame for making any necessary corrections.

Obviously this is an aggressive schedule. There is no reason to feel that these topics and policies cannot be revisited and amended. But it is better to have something in hand to work from than to continuously hope that there will be time to address these issues. A key to the implementation of this process is to trust the ad hoc committee members to do their work well and to utilize the broad array of resources available on the Internet and from other sources.

EMERGENCY
Data Bank

Personnel

Spokesperson for the organization: [contact numbers]

👤 ....

📞 ....

Back-up spokesperson: [contact numbers]

👤 ....

📞 ....

Persons to be called in case of emergency, in order of preference

✚ ....

✚ ....

✚ ....

List staff names, titles, and emergency contact numbers

👤 ....

📞 ....

➕ ....

👤 ....

📞 ....

➕ ....

👤 ....

📞 ....

➕ ....

👤 ....

📞 ....

➕ ....

List board names and emergency contact numbers

👤 ....

➕ ....

👤 ....

➕ ....

👤 ....

➕ ....

Addresses and telephone numbers for any program offices, job sites, and properties

✉ . . . .

☎ . . . .

Media

💬 Talking points for staff answering telephone, attached

▤ Mission statement for the nonprofit

Social media used by the organization

💬 . . . .

Media contact, if one exists

📹 . . . .

📹 Press statement, attached

Corporate

Contacts in larger organization (synods, regional offices, headquarters) and telephone numbers

☎ . . . .

☎ . . . .

☎ . . . .

Bank(s) and contact person

☎ ....

☎ ....

Attorney contact information

👤 ....

☎ ....

Accountant/auditor information

👤 ....

☎ ....

Date of last financial audit ....

Date of last systems audit by emergency team ....

▤ Place where policy manual can be found

About the Author

Starr Mayer is a social worker, mediator and nonprofit executive. Most recently, she worked for over a decade with Habitat for Humanity, serving as the Executive Director of an affiliate in Virginia, the Director of Risk Prevention and Response and a senior advisor on executive transition management. A trained mediator, she has worked with dozens of nonprofits, churches and social service agencies in her 40-year career, with a specialization in dispute resolution and risk management. Her experiences consulting with good people and good organizations in the midst of crises led her to write this book.

Ms. Mayer lives in Gloucester County, Virginia with her husband, Charles. Together they have worked with churches in transition and as mediators. She has two adult sons, two granddaughters, an unruly dog and an overweight cat. She and her husband enjoy sailing and reading.

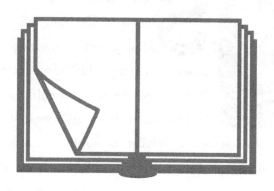

Bibliography

Adams, Tom. *The Nonprofit Leadership Transition and Development Guide: Proven Paths for Leaders and Organizations*. Jossey-Bass, 2010.

Annie E. Casey Foundation. Executive Transition Monographs (Series). http://www.aecf.org/KnowledgeCenter/Publicaions Series/ExecutiveTransitionMonographs.aspx

BoardSource. *The Handbook of Nonprofit Governance*. Jossey-Bass, 2010.

Brooks, David. "Drilling for Certainty." The New York Times, May 27, 2010.

Dewhirst, Scot, and Roberta Mitchell. *The Mediator Handbook: A Training Guide to Mediation Techniques and Skills*. Columbus, Ohio: Center for Dispute Resolution, Capital University Law and Graduate Center, 1990.

Collins, Jim. *Good to Great*. New York: Harper Business, 2001.

Collins, Jim. *Good to Great and the Social Sectors*. New York: Harper Business, 2005.

Drucker, Peter F. *Managing the Nonprofit Organization: Principles and Practices*. New York: Harper Business, 2010.

Halverstadt, Hugh F. *Managing Church Conflict*. Louisville: Westminster/John Knox Press, 1991.

Laughlin, Frederic L., and Robert C. Andringa. *Good Governance for Nonprofits: Developing Principles and Policies for an Effective Board*. Amacom, 2007.

Mancuso, Anthony. *Nonprofit Meetings, Minutes and Records: How to Run Your Nonprofit Corporation So You Don't Run Into Trouble*. NOLO, 2008.

Maravelas, Anna. *How to Reduce Workplace Conflict and Stress*. Franklin Lakes, New Jersey: Career Press, 2005.

Sagawa, Shirley, and Deborah Jospin. *The Charismatic Organization: Eight Ways to Grow a Nonprofit*. Jossey-Bass, 2009.

Wolfred, Tim. *Managing Executive Transitions: A Guide for Nonprofits*. St. Paul, Minnesota: Fieldstone Alliance, 2009.

Welytok, Jill Gilbert and Daniel S. Welytok. *Nonprofit Law and Governance for Dummies*. Wiley Publishing, Inc., 2007.

Additional Resources

BoardSource.org

CompassPoint.com

Nolo.com

TransitionGuides.com

Workplacebullying.org

The author may be contacted at her website
for additional information and support:

starrmayer.com

Endnotes

1   Author's Note: All of the examples in this book are based on real situations and organizations; the details have been changed to hide their identities.

2   Glenn Collins, *New York Times*, September 9, 1997.

3   Jim Collins, *Good to Great* (New York: Harper Business, 2001), 41.

4   Anna Maravelas, *How to Reduce Workplace Conflict and Stress* (New Jersey: Career Press, 2005), 17.

5   Roberta S. Mitchell and Scot E. Dewhirst, *The Mediator's Handbook: A Training Guide to Mediation Techniques and Skills* (Columbus, Ohio: Capital University).

6   www.workplacebullyinginstitute.org